INTRODUCTORY

Read It, Write It

How to write short and extended responses to open-ended questions

S. Dean Wooton

New Readers Press

Read It, Write It Introductory
ISBN 978-1-56420-581-0

New Readers Press
Division of ProLiteracy Worldwide
1320 Jamesville Avenue, Syracuse, New York 13210
www.newreaderspress.com

Printed in the United States of America
9 8 7 6 5 4 3 2 1

All proceeds from the sale of New Readers Press materials support literacy programs in the United States and worldwide.

Developmental Editor: Terrie Lipke
Design and Production Manager: Andrea Woodbury
Cover Designer: Carolyn Boehmer
Production Specialist: Jeffrey R. Smith, Joshua A. Johnson

CONTENTS

UNIT 3

LITERATURE READINGS

PRACTICE TEST

To the Student

Tests are not something that most students look forward to. But they are a fact of school life. Learning test-taking strategies can take some of the worry out of answering test questions. This book will help you learn the strategies you need to write well-constructed responses to open-ended questions.

This book is divided into three units. Each unit uses reading passages from a different subject area: science, social studies, or literature. These are the areas you need to write about most often on tests.

Every lesson begins with a review of a skill or concept. You will practice using concepts such as cause and effect, tone, and sequence. You'll also be shown a simple chart, diagram, or other graphic organizer. It will help you collect and analyze information.

The lesson then guides you step-by-step through the process of reading and answering open-response questions and essay prompts. The strategy follows a four-step plan. You will use this same process whenever you respond to open-ended questions.

Read Read the passage and look for main ideas. Then analyze the question or prompt. Look for key words, such as *describe, explain, compare,* or *define.* These words tell you how to answer the question.

Plan This is a crucial stage in test taking. The lesson provides a graphic organizer and guides you in completing it. Then it walks you through the process of using information from the organizer to plan your writing.

Write Once your planning is done, this step is easy. You will simply put the ideas you've already collected and organized down on paper.

Review and Edit In the final steps of the strategy, you'll check to make sure you've answered the question or prompt completely and accurately. Then you'll check your response for errors in grammar, usage, and spelling. A checklist is provided to help you form the habit of checking the important details. If you don't understand an item on the checklist, mark it and ask your teacher.

Learn this process. Use the passages to practice the strategies until they become automatic. Learning these strategies will give you the confidence to do well on the tests that lie ahead. That will help you succeed in school. And it will give you an advantage now and for years to come.

Lesson 1: Main Idea and Supporting Detai

Develop Your Skills ->

The **main idea** is the most important idea in a paragraph or in a piece of writing. **Supporting details** are facts, opinions, examples, reasons, and other ideas. They explain or describe the main idea.

Every paragraph should have a main idea. All the details in the paragraph should support the main idea. Likewise, a whole passage or longer piece of writing will have a main idea. All the details and paragraph main ideas should support that big idea.

Sometimes the main idea is stated directly. More often, you will have to infer or guess the main idea. To do that, read the passage and list the details. Use a graphic organizer to write the details. Summarize the details and write the main idea.

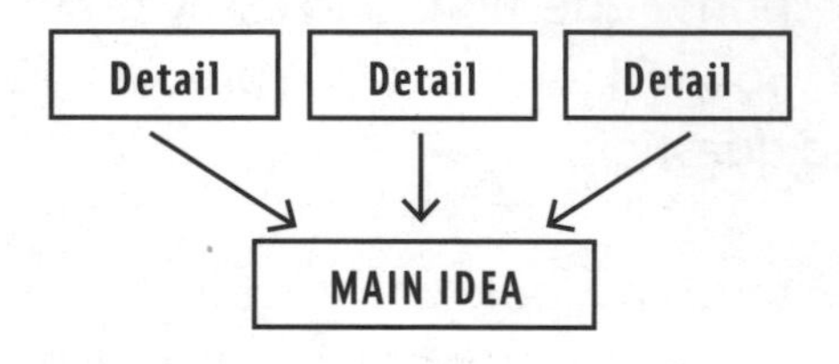

Read ->

LIVING TOGETHER

Crocodiles are some of the most dangerous animals in Africa. They kill several hundred people each year. Countless sheep, cattle, and pigs also get eaten. And yet a small bird will step right into the crocodile's mouth. It's the Egyptian plover. And it survives. In fact, the crocodile seems to welcome the bird. It opens its mouth wide and waits. The bird steps in. Then it pecks around at the crocodile's teeth. It even pecks on its tongue. When the bird is done, it flies off to the next crocodile.

What is happening here is called **symbiosis.** This word describes how some animal and plant species live together. At least one of them benefits. In the case of the crocodile and plover, both animals get something out of it. The crocodile gets its teeth cleaned. And leeches are removed from its tongue. Leeches are a type of worm. They attach themselves to the crocodile's tongue. Then they suck its blood. For its part, the plover gets an easy meal.

There are different kinds of symbiosis. Some, like that between the crocodile and plover, benefit both species. Others are parasitic. An example is the relationship between the crocodile and the leech. A parasite is an animal or plant that lives off another animal or plant. It doesn't give anything in return. Leeches get food from their hosts. Their victims lose blood and may develop an itch.

In another type of symbiosis only one animal benefits. The other animal does not benefit. But it is not hurt either. An example is the relationship between clownfish and sea anemones. Anemones look like plants but are really animals. They live on the sea floor. They protect themselves with stingers. These stingers can kill fish and other small animals. So animals stay away from them. The clownfish, however, isn't hurt by the sting. So the clownfish lives close to the anemone. In that way, it is safe from animals that might want to eat it. The anemone gets nothing from the clownfish. But it is also not hurt by the clownfish.

No one knows how symbiosis happens. It is hard to imagine how a plover would learn that it is safe to walk into a crocodile's mouth.

Write the main idea of this passage. Then give three supporting details. Explain how they support the main idea.

Plan →

This diagram shows two details from the passage. It also states a main idea. Notice that the details are examples of the main idea. Write one more example from the passage.

The plover cleans the crocodile's teeth and gets a meal.	Leeches feed on crocodile blood.	

MAIN IDEA: Symbiosis = a relationship between two species that live together—at least one species benefits.

The model sentences below state two details that support the main idea. Write a sentence adding the detail that you found.

The crocodile lets the plover peck on its teeth and tongue. So the crocodile gets its teeth cleaned, and the plover gets an easy meal. The leech, on the other hand, is a parasite. It takes blood from the crocodile.

Look back at the prompt that follows the reading passage. The next step is to write a sentence that states the main idea of your response. Use words from the prompt. This topic sentence has been written for you. It will be the topic sentence of your essay.

Topic sentence:

The main idea is that some animal species live together in symbiotic relationships.

Write ->

Write your answer to the test prompt below. **Write the main idea of this passage. Then give three supporting details. Explain how they support the main idea.** The answer has been started for you. It begins with the topic sentence.

The main idea is that some animal species live together in symbiotic relationships. The main idea is supported by the following details. The crocodile lets the plover peck on its teeth and tongue.

____

____

____

____

Review and Edit ->

Scoring Standards

Review and revise your writing based on the standards below. Then, check your answer for errors in spelling, grammar, and usage.

Content > Does the response answer the question accurately and completely?

Does it

_____ state the main idea?

_____ identify three supporting details?

_____ explain how the details support the main idea?

_____ include a clear topic sentence?

_____ stay on the topic without including details that do not support the main idea?

Organization > Is the response clearly and logically organized?

Does it

_____ organize ideas so the answer is easy to understand?

Voice and Style > Does the response show skillful use of language?

Does it

_____ display vivid and precise word choices?

_____ use a tone appropriate to the topic and test situation?

Apply Your Skills →

Read →

Millions Fill the Sky

Sometimes the sky seems filled with wings. Millions of orange and black monarch butterflies are arriving at their winter homes. These insects have flown hundreds and thousands of miles. The monarchs migrate from all over North America. *Migrate* means "to travel from one place to another." Monarchs migrate farther than any other insect.

The monarchs make their winter homes in Mexico and California. Monarchs that live east of the Rocky Mountains travel to Mexico. They spend the winters in about 12 sites. Monarchs that live west of the Rocky Mountains migrate to the California coast. They have about 25 sites. The monarchs gather in trees. The winter nesting sites are small. In Mexico sites average seven and a half acres. As a result, each site may have millions of insects.

The monarchs spend about five months in their winter homes. Much of that time, they remain inactive. The monarchs cluster together on tree branches. Each butterfly clings to the branch with its wings hanging over the insect below it. The result is a huge cluster. Each cluster may have hundreds or thousands of insects. The dense clusters help the butterflies stay warm. They also shield them from rain and wind. But sometimes, the insects take flight—thousands of them. Visitors hear the dry clicking of flapping wings. The butterflies almost block the sun.

In March, the monarchs fly north. They head to their summer homes. They waste little time on this trip. They may fly up to 30 miles an hour at times. The monarchs do not breed during their stay in Mexico and California. But when they go north, they breed and lay eggs along the way. The old monarchs die. Their offspring finish the journey north.

During the summer, the monarchs scatter throughout North America. They may breed several times during the summer. These summer monarchs live only a few weeks. Then, as the weather turns cool in the fall, the monarchs fly south again. They do not hurry on this migration. They stop to feed on flowers. They breed and lay eggs. Many of the monarchs that begin the journey south do not finish it. In fact, it may take three generations of monarchs to reach the winter homes. The last generation finishes the journey south. There they will live till spring arrives.

Identify the main idea of the passage. Then explain how each paragraph supports the main idea.

Plan →

This graphic organizer identifies the main idea of the passage. It also gives the main ideas of each of the paragraphs. It shows how the paragraph ideas support the main idea of the passage. Complete the organizer.

Monarch butterflies fly thousands of miles to their winter homes.

Monarchs make their winter homes in California and Mexico.

Monarchs rest during much of their five months in the south.

MAIN IDEA:

Notice how each paragraph tells about monarch butterflies during their migration. Each describes a different time during the migration. Together they explain the whole cycle of the migration.

Write two or three sentences. Explain how two of the paragraphs support the main idea.

Here is a topic sentence for your response. Notice how it uses words from the prompt.

Topic sentence:

The main idea of the passage is that monarchs migrate over great distances.

Write →

Identify the main idea of the passage. Then explain how each paragraph supports the main idea.

Scoring Standards

Your answer will be scored based on the standards below. Review your writing. If it doesn't meet the standards, you won't receive the highest score. Revise to improve your response. If necessary, rewrite it on another piece of paper.

Content > Does the response answer the question accurately and completely?

Does it

______ state the main idea of the passage?
______ explain how the main ideas in each of the paragraphs support the main idea of the passage?
______ include a clear topic sentence?
______ provide enough details to support the topic sentence?
______ stay on the topic without including details that do not support the main idea?

Organization > Is the response clearly and logically organized?

Does it

______ present ideas in an order that makes the answer easy to understand?
______ include transitions to make the relationships among ideas clear?

Voice and Style > Does the response show skillful use of language?

Does it

______ display vivid and precise word choices?
______ use a variety of sentence structures, such as simple, compound, and complex sentences?
______ use a tone appropriate to the topic and test situation?

Use this checklist to proofread your answer. Correct any mechanical errors.

Mechanics

______ capitalization
______ punctuation
______ spelling
______ sentence fragments
______ subject-verb agreement
______ consistency of verb tenses
______ paragraphing
______ run-on sentences

Lesson 2:

Summary

Develop Your Skills ->

A **summary** is a brief statement of the main ideas and important details in a piece of writing. A summary is different from a paraphrase. A paraphrase restates what is said but in different words. It is usually about as long as the original passage. A summary includes only the most important ideas. It is always shorter than the passage.

You have already reviewed the skill of finding main ideas and supporting details. Build on this skill to develop a summary. First read the passage. Use a chart like the one below. Write the main idea of each paragraph or section along with the most important details. To write your summary, first summarize the main ideas in a topic sentence. Then restate the details in your own words. Show how they connect to the topic sentence.

MAIN IDEAS	MOST IMPORTANT DETAILS
Main Idea 1	Detail 1
	Detail 2
	Detail 3
Main Idea 2	Detail 1
	Detail 2
	Detail 3

Read ->

Space Tourists

1 Would you like to travel into space as a tourist? In 2001, the Russian space agency took an American millionaire into space. His name was Dennis Tito. He spent six days on the International Space Station. He was the first space tourist. Russia charged him $20 million for the trip.

2 The space station is a joint effort of several countries. NASA is the United States' space agency. NASA didn't like the idea of a tourist on the station. But they agreed to Tito's visit. NASA knew Russia

needed the money for their space program. Besides, NASA isn't opposed to space tourism. In fact, the agency thinks space tourism could be worth billions of dollars.

3 Some people say we should have space tourism. It's a good way to promote the space program. It gets average people thinking about space. Then they will support the program. Of course, it will be a long time before the average person can afford a trip into space. But for now, rich tourists like Tito will help pay the costs.

4 But other people ask if tourists should go into space. Is now the right time? Should we let them risk their lives in space? Should we let tourists put astronauts in danger?

5 The answers are no. The U.S. space program is no place for tourists. Space travel is dangerous for anyone. That includes tourists and astronauts alike. A small mistake can spell disaster. Plus, there are no safety, training, or health standards. Tourists may spend a few weeks learning basics. But that is little help. The astronauts must still take care of them. And the tourists are a nuisance. Besides being underfoot, tourists keep the astronauts from doing their job, which is research. When Tito went into space, NASA delayed some work aboard the space station. There were too many dangers involved to do high-risk tasks with him there.

6 Space travel for average people is a great dream. It should be our goal to bring space travel within reach of everyone. But the time isn't now. Let's wait until space travel can be made safe for the untrained tourist.

Summarize paragraph 5. Include four important details from the paragraph.

Plan →

Before you begin writing, look at the chart. It shows the main idea from paragraph 5. It also shows two of the most important details. Complete the chart by adding two more important details. To find the details, ask yourself: What ideas most help me understand the main idea of this paragraph?

MAIN IDEA OF PARAGRAPH 5	MOST IMPORTANT DETAILS
Space is no place for tourists.	Space travel is dangerous.
	There are no safety, training, or health standards for space tourists.

The sample sentence below shows how the first detail might be restated in a summary. Add a sentence about the second detail.

Space travel is dangerous for anyone who is out there.

______

______

Now write sentences about the two details you added to the chart.

______

______

______

Look back at the prompt that follows the reading passage. Write a sentence that states the main idea of your response. Use words from the prompt. This will be the topic sentence of your essay. This topic sentence has been written for you.

Topic sentence:

There are many reasons why tourists should not travel in space.

Write →

Summarize paragraph 5. Include four important details from the paragraph.
Write your response to the test prompt below.

There are many reasons why tourists should not travel in space.
First of all, space travel is dangerous for anyone who is out there.

Remember, include only the most important details in a summary. Other details may be interesting, but they may not be important enough for the summary.

Review and Edit →

Scoring Standards

Review and revise your writing based on the standards below. Then, check your answer for errors in spelling, grammar, and usage.

Content > Does the response answer the question accurately and completely?
Does it
_____ state the main idea of the paragraph?
_____ include the four most important details?
_____ include a clear topic sentence?
_____ display vivid and precise word choices?
_____ restate ideas in your own words?

Organization > Is the response clearly and logically organized?
Does it
_____ organize ideas so the answer is easy to understand?

Voice and Style > Does the response show skillful use of language?
Does it
_____ display vivid and precise word choices?
_____ use a tone appropriate to the topic and test situation?

Apply Your Skills →

Read →

Energy in the Wind

This country runs on energy. It heats and cools our homes and cooks our meals. It makes our clothing and cars, and it lights our streets. It's no wonder that people are searching for the cheapest, most plentiful ways of making energy. In recent years, engineers have learned to make electricity from the wind. The wind is free. This sounds like the perfect answer, right? Perhaps, but it might surprise you to learn that many groups of people oppose wind power. And they have some strong arguments.

If you think of charming Dutch windmills when you think of wind power, think again. Today's wind turbines are industrial power plants. A *turbine* is a machine that changes one kind of energy into another kind. A wind turbine changes wind into electricity. It looks like a huge airplane propeller mounted on a tower. Many of today's towers are 400 feet high. Some are even higher.

And energy companies don't usually build just one turbine here and there. They build hundreds of them at a time. They call them "wind farms." Wind farms have many of the problems of any other industrial site.

Imagine for a moment a lovely valley with a long tree-covered mountain range beyond it. Now imagine the mountain stripped of its trees along the ridge. (That's the best place for wind.) In place of the trees are hundreds of 400-foot wind turbines. Roads have been cut across the hillside so service trucks can reach each turbine. In addition, more towers have been put up. These stretch in a row down the valley as far as you can see. Power lines link these towers to the wind turbines on the ridge. They deliver the electricity to homes and businesses.

Now stand back and listen. From several hundred yards away, you can hear the whoosh of the blades and the humming of the turbines. The sound isn't deafening. But if you expected to hear the quiet sounds of nature, the turbines may annoy you.

It's a fact that wind turbines

sometimes kill birds. In California, hundreds of rare birds of prey have been killed when they flew into the blades and towers of wind turbines. But it is also true that many birds die flying into the smokestacks of coal-burning power plants.

Wind energy is not a perfect answer to all our energy needs. The questions we must ask ourselves, however, are these. First, what are our choices? We cannot do without energy. Do we keep using coal and natural gas to make electricity? They create dangerous pollution. That causes health problems. It also causes changes in our climate. The pollutants keep heat from escaping the planet. As a result, the earth is getting warmer. The ice caps are melting. Some places are becoming drier. Weather patterns are changing. The changing climate may affect farming. Good farmlands may become less productive.

Compared to the problems caused by coal and gas, wind energy doesn't look so bad. It's not a perfect answer. But there may not be one. Energy from the wind may be our best choice.

Write a summary of the passage. Include at least eight details.

Plan →

This chart lists main ideas and important details from the passage. Use the chart to gather details for your summary. Complete the organizer.

MAIN IDEA OF PASSAGE:	
Wind energy has problems, but it's our best way to make electricity.	
MAIN IDEAS OF PARAGRAPHS	**MOST IMPORTANT DETAILS**
Main Idea 1: Wind energy has problems.	• 400-foot towers, huge propellers • hundreds of turbines on a wind farm • roads to service the turbines • •
Main Idea 2:	• coal and gas cause pollution • • •

The sentences below restate the first two details. Write sentences to restate the next two details. Use your own words.

The problems with wind turbines are like those for most other industrial sites.

Each turbine has a 400-foot tower with a huge propeller.

Write a topic sentence for your summary. State the main idea of the passage in your words.

Topic sentence:

Write →

Write a summary of the passage. Start with your topic sentence. Include at least eight details.

Scoring Standards

Your answer will be scored based on the standards below. Review your writing. If it doesn't meet the standard, you won't receive the highest score. Revise to improve your response. If necessary, rewrite it on another piece of paper.

Content > Does the response answer the question accurately and completely?

Does it

_____ state the main idea of the paragraph?
_____ include a clear topic sentence?
_____ restate ideas in your own words?
_____ include at least eight of the most important details?

Organization > Is the response clearly and logically organized?

Does it

_____ present ideas in an order that makes the answer easy to understand?
_____ include transitions to make the relationships among ideas clear?

Voice and Style > Does the response show skillful use of language?

Does it

_____ display vivid and precise word choices?
_____ use a variety of sentence structures, such as simple, compound, and complex sentences?
_____ use a tone appropriate to the topic and test situation?

Now, check your writing against the editing checklist below.

Mechanics

_____ capitalization
_____ punctuation
_____ spelling
_____ sentence fragments
_____ subject-verb agreement
_____ consistency of verb tenses
_____ paragraphing
_____ run-on sentences

Lesson 3:

Sequence

Develop Your Skills ->

Sequence is the order in which events happen. Knowing the sequence helps you understand how events are related and why an event is important. Often events are reported in the order they happen. But sometimes, the events are described out of order.

Writers signal the sequence of events. Sometimes they give dates or times. They also use transitional words such as *while, next,* and *before* to tell the order of events.

To create a sequence chart, find the first event that happens. Write it down and draw a box around it. Then add the next event to the chain, and so on. Be aware that sometimes two or more events happen at the same time.

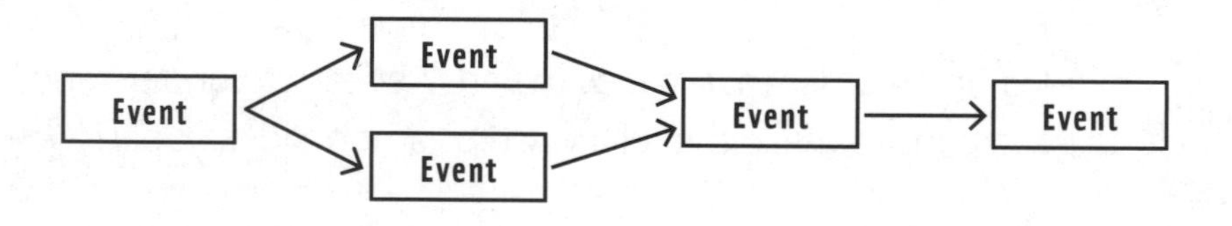

Read ->

Falling Objects

Aristotle said that a heavy object falls faster than a light object. And the heavier the object, the faster it falls. Aristotle lived in ancient Greece from about 384 to 322 BC.

For hundreds of years, most people accepted Aristotle's statement. It made sense. The weight of an object is what makes an object fall to earth. Or so they reasoned. So a heavier object will fall faster than a lighter object. This all seems very logical.

But other people thought differently. It made sense to them that all objects fall at the same speed. If a large rock and a small rock are thrown into the air, they fall at the same rate. Right? A few people did tests. They tried to show what really happens. But the results were questioned. So the argument raged on.

Then in 1590, Galileo Galilei entered the debate. According to legend, he took a cannonball and a musket ball to the top of the Leaning Tower of Pisa. This tower, which is in Pisa, Italy, leans to the side. So the balls could be dropped and not hit the side of the building. Galileo and a helper dropped the balls at the same instant. The balls fell 185 feet to the ground. And they landed at exactly the same moment. A large crowd witnessed the event.

Since that time, most scientists have agreed. All objects fall at the same rate. Their size and weight do not matter. It became part of the law of gravity. Exceptions, of course, include things like a feather and a cannonball. The cannonball falls faster. However, it falls faster because air holds up the feather. If there were no air—for example on the moon—the objects would fall at the same rate.

But a question arose. Does gravity have the same effect on even the smallest objects? Will an atom, for example, fall as fast as a cannonball? In the 1990s, Steven Chu of Stanford University found a way to answer this question. He proved that objects as small as a single atom follow the law of gravity. These tiny objects fall at the same rate as every other object.

In the 1990s, Steven Chu proved that atoms fall at the same rate as much heavier objects. What events led to Chu's discovery?

Plan →

People learned about gravity over a period of time. This sequence chart shows some of those events in the order they happened. Add events from the passage to complete the chart.

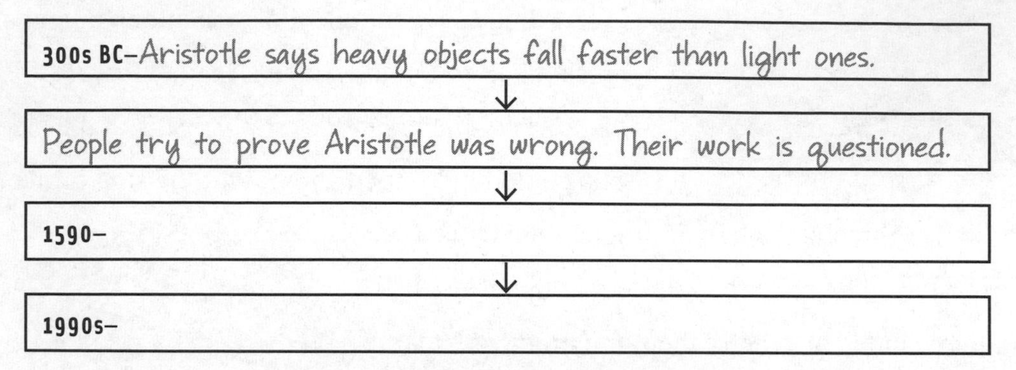

The sample sentences below describe the sequence of the first two events. Write one or two more sentences. Describe the third event. Use a transitional word or other clue to show how it is connected to the second event.

In the fourth century BC, Aristotle said that heavier objects fall faster than lighter objects. Later, some people disagreed with Aristotle. But none of their experiments were convincing.

Now describe the final event. Make it clear how it fits the sequence of events.

Look back at the question that follows the reading passage. Write a sentence that states the main idea of your answer. Use words from the prompt. This will be the topic sentence of your essay. This topic sentence has been written for you.

Topic sentence:

Chu's discovery followed the work of other scientists.

Write →

In the 1990s, Steven Chu proved that atoms fall at the same rate as much heavier objects. What events led up to Chu's discovery? The answer has been started for you. Complete the answer to the test question below.

Choose transitional words to make the order of events clear.

first	**after**
during	**while**
next	**last**
then	**finally**

Chu's discovery followed the work of other scientists. In the fourth century BC, Aristotle said that heavier objects fall faster than lighter objects.

____

____

____

____

____

Review and Edit →

Scoring Standards

Review and revise your writing based on the standards below. Then, check your answer for errors in spelling, grammar, and usage.

Content > Does the response answer the question accurately and completely?

Does it

______ describe the sequence of events?
______ include a clear topic sentence?
______ stay on the topic without including details that do not support the main idea?

Organization > Is the response clearly and logically organized?

Does it

______ organize ideas so the answer is easy to understand?
______ include transitions to make the sequence of events clear?

Voice and Style > Does the response show skillful use of language?

Does it

______ display vivid and precise word choices?
______ use a tone appropriate to the topic and test situation?

Apply Your Skills –>

Read –>

Galloping Gertie

The Tacoma Narrows Bridge was completed near the city of Tacoma, Washington, in 1940. It was an engineering marvel. It was a suspension bridge. That means the roadway was hung from cables, which were connected to tall towers. The Tacoma Narrows Bridge was the third longest suspension bridge in the world. It also had the longest single span of any bridge in the country.

But the Tacoma Narrows Bridge became even more famous four months after it was finished. That's when the bridge collapsed.

Begun in 1938, the bridge began showing signs of problems even before it was finished. On windy days, the roadway would move in wavelike motions. The movement became worse when the bridge was finished. On windy days, it had a roller coaster effect. It was so bad that drivers sometimes lost sight of cars farther ahead as the bridge swayed up and down. Motorists called the bridge "Galloping Gertie."

Engineers began looking for a way to fix the problem. But they couldn't come up with a solution. The problem had to do with the roadway itself. It caught too much wind.

On November 7, 1940, winds of 42 miles per hour raced through the Narrows. The bridge began swaying more and more. Then it began to twist and corkscrew. At times, one side of the bridge was 28 feet higher than the other side.

Leonard Coatsworth was an editor for a Tacoma newspaper. He was caught on the bridge when it began to fall. He gave a firsthand account of what happened. "Just as I drove past the towers," he wrote, "the bridge began to sway violently from side to side. Before I realized it, the tilt became so violent that I lost control of the car." Coatsworth stopped the car and got out. He was immediately thrown to the ground by the violent motion. "Around me I could hear concrete cracking." Coatsworth tried to stand up but was thrown down again. Meanwhile, his car began to slide back and forth on the bridge.

"On hands and knees most of the time," he reported, "I crawled 500 yards or more to the towers . . . My breath was coming in gasps; my knees were raw and bleeding, my hands bruised and swollen from gripping the concrete curb." Finally, he once more risked standing. He ran to the end of the bridge. Just as he reached safety, he turned. "I saw the bridge in its final collapse and saw my car plunge into the Narrows."

After the bridge fell, engineers studied what happened. They used the knowledge to design a new Tacoma Narrows bridge. A model of the new bridge was created. It was placed in a wind tunnel so the effect of the wind could be studied. This work helped engineers learn how to predict how bridges respond to wind. It was important work. It has helped engineers around the world build safer bridges.

What happened to the Tacoma Narrows Bridge? Describe five or more events in the order they happened.

Plan →

The following chart shows the sequence of events that is described in the passage. Complete the sequence chart.

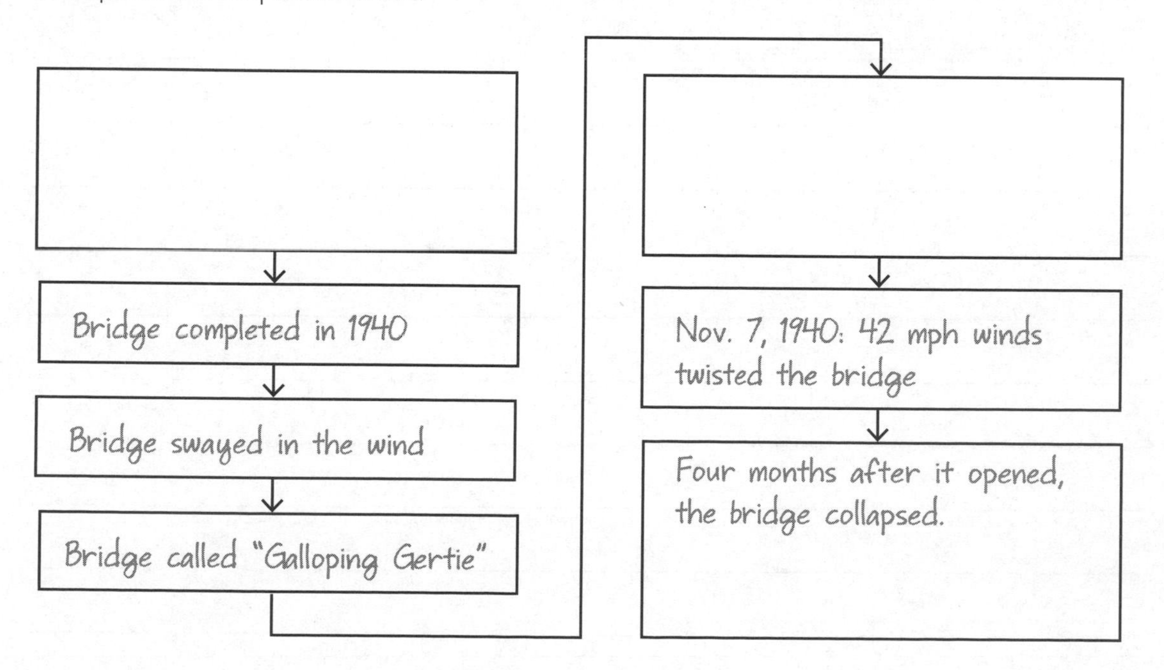

This sentence describes the sequence of two of the events.

When motorists crossed the bridge, they noticed it swaying in the wind. They called it "Galloping Gertie."

Write a sentence to describe the sequence of the first two events shown on the diagram. Use transitional words or dates to make the sequence clear.

Write a topic sentence stating the main idea of your response to the question.

Topic sentence:

Write →

Write your answer to the question. **What happened to the Tacoma Narrows Bridge? Describe five or more events in the order they happened.**

Review and Edit ->

Scoring Standards

Your answer will be scored based on the standards below. Review your writing. If it doesn't meet the standard, you won't receive the highest score. Revise to improve your response. If necessary, rewrite it on another piece of paper.

Content > Does the response answer the question accurately and completely?

Does it

_____ describe the sequence of events?

_____ include a clear topic sentence?

_____ provide enough details to support the topic sentence?

_____ stay on the topic without including details that do not support the main idea?

Organization > Is the response clearly and logically organized?

Does it

_____ present ideas in an order that makes the answer easy to understand?

_____ include transitions to make the sequence of events clear?

Voice and Style > Does the response show skillful use of language?

Does it

_____ display vivid and precise word choices?

_____ use a variety of sentence structures, such as simple, compound, and complex sentences?

_____ use a tone appropriate to the topic and test situation?

Now, check your writing against the editing checklist below.

Mechanics

_____ capitalization

_____ punctuation

_____ spelling

_____ sentence fragments

_____ subject-verb agreement

_____ consistency of verb tenses

_____ paragraphing

_____ run-on sentences

Invasion of the Fire Ants

If you live or travel in the southern United States, you may meet one of the most vicious, dangerous insects in the world. It's the fire ant. Red fire ants are tiny. They measure about three millimeters (one-tenth of an inch) in length. But what they lack in size, they make up for in numbers and viciousness. Step on a mound and in seconds a swarm of thousands of ants emerge. And they will gang up on anything that's nearby. Small animals are killed by fire ants. People have been so badly hurt they've had to go to the hospital. Some have even died.

Fire ants don't do most of their damage by biting. They sting like wasps. As they sting, they inject a poison. Some people are made sick by the poison, just as they are by wasp and bee stings. When attacked by thousands of ants, a victim may receive thousands of stings.

Actually, there are four different types of fire ants in the United States. Two are native, or natural, to the United States. Two are newcomers from South America. The native fire ants are not much of a problem. And one of the newcomers, the black fire ant, is not a big problem. It has not spread widely. That may be because it cannot compete with the red fire ant. This fourth member of the family—the red fire ant— is a vicious killer.

Remember the steps:

Read
Plan
Write
Review & Edit

The first red fire ants arrived in the United States in the 1930s. They came from South America on ships. Their first stop was Mobile, Alabama. From there, they've spread through most of the southeastern United States. They've also made their way west into New Mexico and even to California. So far, they haven't spread much farther north than central Arkansas and southern Tennessee. They probably can't survive hard winters, so they may not spread much farther north than their current range.

Fire ants spread in several ways. They spread naturally during mating flights. Males and females have wings. And they mate in the air. After mating, the female lands and starts a new colony or ant community, usually some distance from where she was born. Sometimes, an entire colony will move. The ants also spread during floods. Then they form themselves into a living raft. The floodwaters may carry colonies miles away. They infest a new area when they strike land. But fire ants are chiefly spread by people. After World War II, people began buying grass sod and other plants used for landscaping.

Fire ants lived in the soil. When the plants moved, so did the ants. Often, they got a free ride of hundreds of miles. As a result, the ants spread into eight southern states. In 1958, the government began controlling the movement of landscape plants. But it was too late.

Once fire ants reach a new home, they populate it quickly. When a new queen starts a colony on her own, it grows slowly at first. She lays ten or fifteen eggs. In about a week, they hatch. These first ants are very small. And they are all workers. They do not lay eggs. They only build the nest and feed the queen. Meanwhile, the queen lays more eggs. Larger workers emerge, and the colony starts growing. They begin building a mound. Every day, more workers are born. Within six months, the colony will have several thousand ants. And it will keep growing. There is usually only one queen in a colony. But she will live about seven years. During that time, she will lay about 1,600 eggs every day. An established fire ant colony may have 250,000 ants.

Typically, fire ants live in large mounds. An average mound will be about one and a half feet in diameter and ten inches high. But if the soil is heavier, it can be over three feet high. There are no entrances into the mound. Instead, tunnels connect to the ground around the mound. When the mound is disturbed, ants emerge from all around. They swarm onto the intruder, stinging viciously.

The mound has three purposes. First, the mound absorbs heat, keeping the ants warm. Second, it raises the ant colony above the surrounding ground. This keeps it from flooding during heavy rain. Third, it serves as a take-off point when new males and females are ready to leave the nest and mate.

Although fire ants typically do build mounds, mounds are not necessary. When they find the right situation, ants may build nests in rotten trees, the walls of buildings, and even under sidewalks.

Federal, state, and local governments are at war with fire ants. But there's little chance that we'll ever get rid of the fire ant. At best, we'll contain it and keep it from taking over. So don't go poking around in anthills. You may find more ants that you expect.

1. Are all fire ants serious pests? Explain your answer.

2. Describe fire ant nests. Include details that explain what the nests look like and where they are found.

3. **Fire ants have become a major pest over a large part of the United States. What makes fire ants such a big problem?**

____

____

____

____

____

____

____

____

____

____

____

____

____

____

Checklist

Content, Organization, and Style

_____ Accurate, complete response
_____ Main idea
_____ Supporting details
_____ Topic sentence
_____ Logical organization
_____ Vivid, precise word choices
_____ Appropriate tone

Spelling, Grammar, and Usage

_____ Capitalization
_____ Punctuation
_____ Spelling
_____ Fragments and run-on sentences
_____ Subject and verb agreement
_____ Consistent verb tenses
_____ Correct paragraphs

Why We Should Travel into Space

1 Traveling into space is expensive. President George W. Bush said sending a space mission to Mars might cost a trillion dollars. The average shuttle mission costs about $1.3 billion. The Hubble Space Telescope cost $1.5 billion to put into space. And it costs $250 million every year to maintain it. Some people say this is too much. We should spend our money on problems here on Earth. There are people who cannot afford health care. Our schools and colleges need more support. Our taxes are already too high. So why waste money on space? What do we get from it? Is learning about the planets and stars worth that much money? The answer is, yes! And here are some reasons why.

2 Right now, Earth is our only home. And the earth has many problems. Global warming may reduce our ability to grow food. Pollution is poisoning our air. And it may get worse. Maybe you don't think these problems are that serious. Maybe they won't get bad enough to kill us. But what about overpopulation? The number of people living on earth is increasing by over 74 million each year. That's more than 6 million extra mouths to feed every month. How long can we feed and care for all these people? Another fifty years? A hundred years? Sooner or later, events will catch up with us. Earth will no longer be able to give us all a home and enough to eat. Then, what will we do? Where will we go?

3 A giant meteor crashed into Earth 65 million years ago. The blast threw toxic chemicals into the air. It created a cloud of dust. The dust kept the sun from reaching Earth for six months. Plants died off. So animals didn't have enough to eat. And because the dust blocked the sun, Earth got colder. Ice covered large parts of the planet. It was a long, harsh winter. Many animals didn't live through it. Among those that didn't make it were the dinosaurs. What if such a disaster strikes Earth again? What would we do? With an advanced space program, we might be able to see such a disaster coming. We could prepare. Perhaps we could destroy the meteor before it reached Earth. Perhaps we could leave the planet until the danger passed.

4 These are all things that might drive us into space. But there are reasons we should want to go as well. We spend millions of dollars to mine for coal, oil, natural gas, iron, and other minerals. And our supplies are running out. In space, there are more fuels and other minerals than we can ever use.

5 We also benefit just from trying to explore space. The space program of the 1950s and 1960s gives us many examples. For instance, we take for granted the use of satellites. Some help us predict the weather. They chart the paths of storms. Other satellites carry TV and radio broadcasts. All these satellites grew out of the early space effort.

6 So our efforts in space have given us useful new tools. And they have also helped our economy. For example, for every dollar spent on satellites, the economy grew by more than 25 dollars. Even today, many people are working to apply what we have learned from our space program to everyday life.

7 But there's one more reason to go into space. And maybe it's the most important one. We should go into space because that's where our curiosity leads us. Humans have succeeded because we have always wanted to learn more and do more. We have always wanted to go beyond the next mountain or river just to see what is there. That curiosity led humans to find the western hemisphere. It led the pioneers to cross the Appalachian Mountains and the Mississippi River. Space—we need to go there because it's out there.

8 So why should we go into space? The answers are easy. We should go there because it makes sense and because we need to learn about it. And we should go there because as humans we cannot and should not stop exploring and learning.

1. Write a summary of paragraph 2. Include five important details.

2. Write a summary of paragraphs 4, 5, and 6. Include four important details.

3. Write a summary of the passage. Include at least eight important details.

____

____

____

____

____

____

____

____

____

____

____

____

____

____

Checklist

Content, Organization, and Style

_____ Accurate, complete response
_____ Main idea
_____ Most important details
_____ Ideas restated in your own words
_____ Topic sentence
_____ Logical organization
_____ Vivid, precise word choices
_____ Appropriate tone

Spelling, Grammar, and Usage

_____ Capitalization
_____ Punctuation
_____ Spelling
_____ Fragments and run-on sentences
_____ Subject and verb agreement
_____ Consistent verb tenses
_____ Correct paragraphs

Flight

Since the earliest times, humans have dreamed of flying. The ancient Greeks created a myth about human flight. In it, Icarus was given wings made of feathers and wax. Icarus soared into the air. But the joy of flight was too much for him. He flew too high and too close to the sun. His wings melted. Icarus fell into the sea and drowned. The myth foretold the future of flight for centuries. There were many attempts at flight. But all ended in failure.

Leonardo da Vinci was one of the first people to seriously study flying. He was a famous Italian artist and inventor. In the 1480s, he drew more than one hundred sketches of flying machines. One drawing shows a flying machine with wings that flap. The power is provided by a man pumping the wings. Another sketch shows a machine that looks like a helicopter. As far as we know, none of da Vinci's machines were ever built. Modern designers say they would not have worked. Humans are not strong enough to power them.

There were many other attempts at flight. Some were serious, some humorous, and some dangerous. All failed. Then two bicycle mechanics tried their luck. They built a plane and put an engine in it. In 1903, they flew it for 12 seconds at Kitty Hawk, North Carolina. These were the Wright brothers. They were the first to build and fly an airplane.

After that, planes became bigger and faster. People began traveling across countries. They flew around the world. But one dream still escaped them. Humans still could not fly under their own power.

In 1959, Henry Kremer offered a prize. Kremer was a businessperson. He would give the prize to the first person who built a human-powered airplane. To win the prize, the plane had to fly a one-mile course in the shape of a figure eight.

In the mid-1970s, an inventor named Paul MacCready set out to win the prize. He solved all the problems that had defeated those who came before him.

The biggest problem was powering the plane. MacCready provided power with a machine like a bicycle. The pilot pedaled it. But humans are not very strong. A hang glider, for example, is a very light flying machine. It can fly a long time by riding air currents. But sooner or later, it will come to earth. To keep flying, it needs an engine. It must produce about one and a half horsepower. A strong bicyclist can produce only about one-half horsepower. MacCready had to get more power from his pilot. Or he had to reduce the need for power.

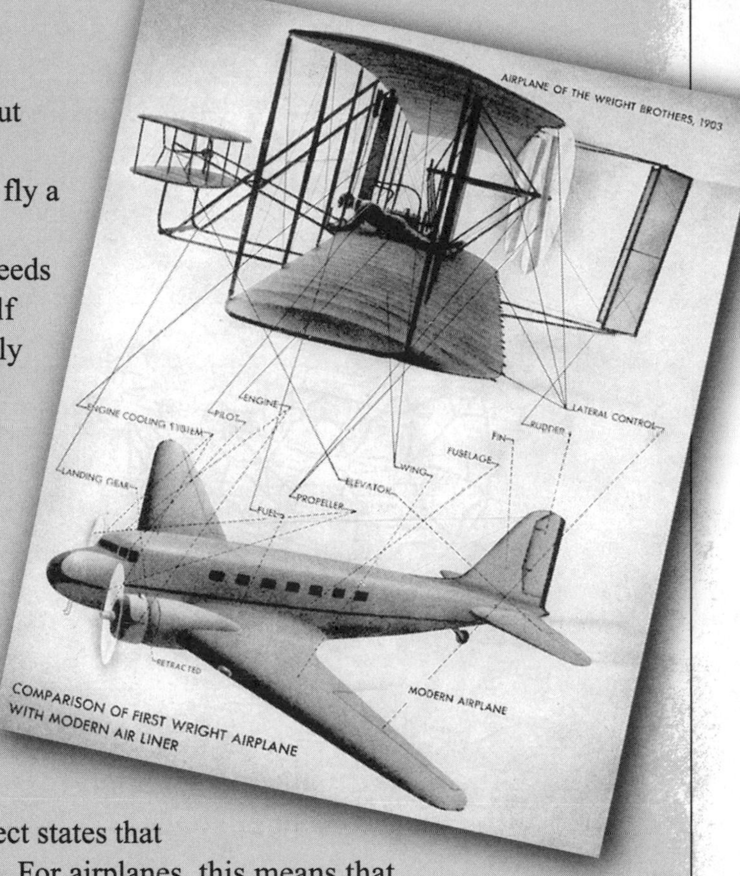

MacCready had some ideas. First, he used very light materials. His plane weighed just 70 pounds. He called it the *Gossamer Condor.*

Second, he made the most of the Bernoulli effect. The Bernoulli effect is one of the basics of flight. It is named for Daniel Bernoulli, a Swiss mathematician. He published his work in 1738. The Bernoulli effect states that the faster a fluid moves the less pressure it has. For airplanes, this means that when air flows faster over the top of a wing than over the bottom, the plane lifts into the air. This is because there is less pressure on the top than on the bottom. So the plane is pulled upward.

Airplane engineers design their wings to create the Bernoulli effect. They give the top of the wing more curve than the bottom. That makes the air flow faster across the top than it flows across the bottom. MacCready made the wings of the *Condor* 96 feet long. And they were curved to give the plane the most lift.

A bicycle rider hung below the wings. As long as he could keep the *Condor* moving forward, the wings would pull the *Condor* upward, keeping it in flight. The plane was light. So the pilot could pedal fast enough to keep it in the air. MacCready had solved both problems.

In 1977, the *Condor* won the prize. It flew just ten feet off the ground. And it flew barely 10 miles an hour. But it finished the figure-eight course. It proved that human-powered flight was possible. In the years that followed, MacCready won other prizes for human-powered flight. One of his planes, the *Gossamer Albatross,* flew across the English Channel. That's a distance of about 30 miles.

1. **What happened to Icarus when he tried to fly? Describe five events in the order they happened.**

2. **There were many real attempts to learn to fly. Describe three of these events in the order they happened.**

3. What problems did MacCready have to solve before he achieved human-powered flight? Explain the problems and how he solved them.

____

____

____

____

____

____

____

____

____

____

____

____

____

____

Checklist

Content, Organization, and Style
______ Accurate, complete response
______ Sequence of events clear
______ Topic sentence
______ Supporting details
______ Logical organization
______ Transitional words
______ Vivid, precise word choices
______ Appropriate tone

Spelling, Grammar, and Usage
______ Capitalization
______ Punctuation
______ Spelling
______ Fragments and run-on sentences
______ Subject and verb agreement
______ Consistent verb tenses
______ Correct paragraphs

Lesson 4:

Cause and Effect

Develop Your Skills ->

Cause and effect shows how two or more events are related. They can be related in different ways. For example, causes and effects can form a chain as each effect becomes the cause of some new effect. A cause can have one effect or many. An effect can be the result of more than one cause. These diagrams show some of the ways causes and effects can be related. Notice how an effect becomes a cause when it makes something else happen.

Don't confuse sequence with cause and effect. Just because one event comes before another does not mean the first event caused the second event to happen. Some cause and effect relationships are signaled by transitional words such as *so* and *because.*

Cause-and-Effect Chain

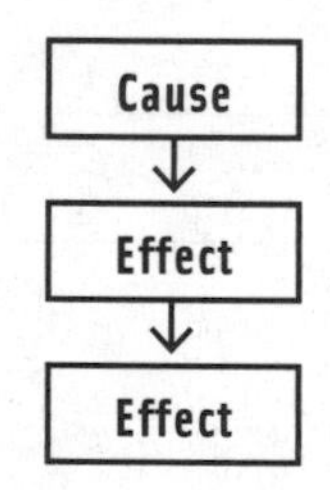

Cause with Several Effects

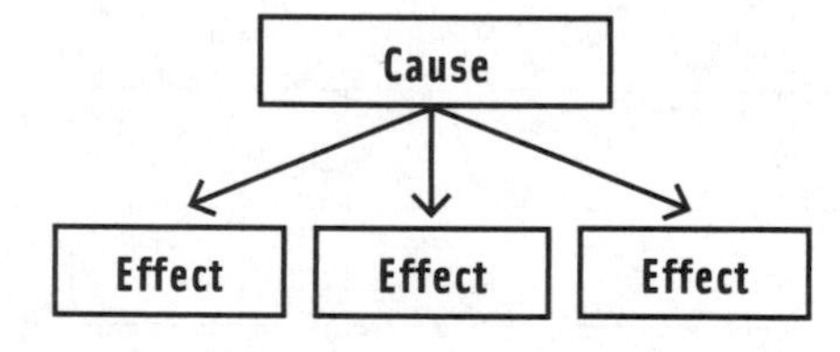

Effect with Several Causes

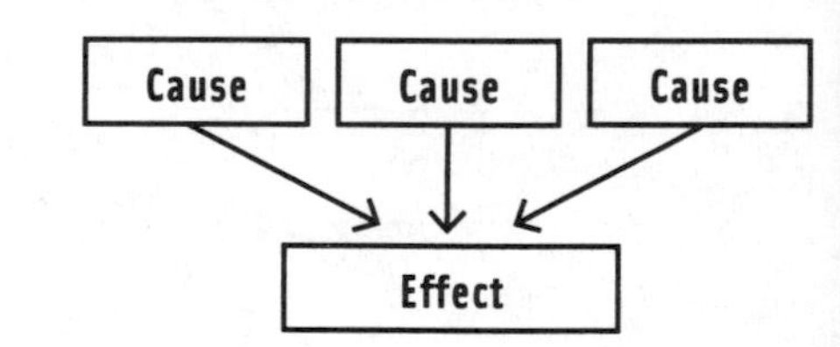

Read ->

THEY PANICKED OVER RADIO

On Sunday evening, October 30, 1938, about 12 million people tuned in to listen to a radio play. (This was before the days of television.) What they heard became the most famous radio program in broadcast history.

At the time, Orson Welles was head of *Mercury Theatre on the Air.* The program ran at the same time as the *Chase and Sanborn Hour,* the most popular program on radio. Welles wanted more listeners. So he helped rewrite a book as a radio play. The book was *War of the Worlds,* by H. G. Wells.

At 8:00 P.M., Welles went on the air. First, he introduced the play and set the scene. A weather report followed. Then a music program began. All of this was part of the play.

Soon after the music began, a reporter broke in with a news bulletin. He said that explosions had been seen on Mars. The music then returned for a few minutes. Then there was another alert. A reporter talked with a scientist. While he was speaking, someone handed him a note. It said that some huge object had struck Earth in New Jersey. The scientist thought it might be a meteorite.

These bulletins seemed normal to listeners. Radio stations often broke into broadcasts to report news. And these alerts sounded like live reports.

The music returned. But more bulletins followed as additional objects struck Earth. The reporter went to the scene. A large metal tube had been found. It slowly opened, and things "wiggled" out. They were Martians, and they were invading Earth! Soldiers were called out. Fighting grew intense. Each news report told of the battle spreading.

Some listeners thought these events were really happening. About one million Americans panicked. They called police and radio stations. Some people hid in basements with loaded guns. Others packed their cars and fled. Some deaths were even reported. But none were ever proved to have occurred.

Welles didn't try to frighten people. But he didn't remind listeners often enough that the program was fiction. The first reminder occurred an hour into the play. Many people didn't hear it.

After the panic, Welles said he was sorry. "I don't think we will choose anything like this again," he said. And then he expressed surprise at what happened. "It was our thought that perhaps people might be bored or annoyed at hearing" such an unlikely tale.

Orson Welles wanted to make a popular radio program. He ended up making broadcast history. How did this happen?

Plan →

This diagram states that Welles presented *War of the Worlds* in a realistic way. Then it shows that the listeners panicked because the play was presented. Several more things happened because they panicked. Write these effects in the open boxes in the diagram.

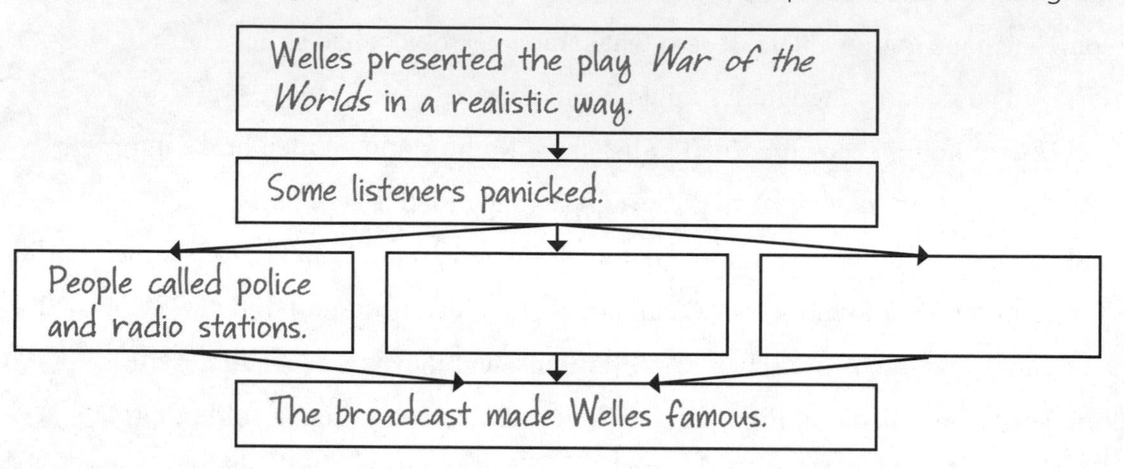

Look at the diagram. The sample sentences tell how the first two events are related. Write a sentence that explains the first effect of the panic.

Welles presented the play *War of the Worlds* in a realistic way. Because it was so realistic, about one million listeners panicked. They thought Martians were really invading Earth.

Now write one or more sentences describing the effects you added to the diagram. Tell how they were caused.

Look back at the question that follows the reading passage. Write a sentence that states the main idea of your answer. Use words from the prompt. This will be the topic sentence of your essay. This topic sentence has been written for you.

Topic sentence:

Because Orson Welles wanted to make a popular radio program, he produced *War of the Worlds* in a realistic way.

Write ->

Choose transitional words to explain how causes and effects are related.

as a result	consequently
because	then
therefore	when
effect	so
since	cause

Orson Welles wanted to produce a popular radio program. He ended up making broadcast history. How did this happen? The answer has been started for you. Use the events on your diagram to complete the answer.

Because Orson Welles wanted to make a popular radio program, he produced War of the Worlds in a realistic way. The program told about the invasion of Earth by Martians. Because it was so realistic, about one million listeners panicked. They thought Martians were really invading Earth.

Review and Edit ->

Scoring Standards

Review and revise your writing based on the standards below. Then, check your answer for errors in spelling, grammar, and usage.

Content > Does the response answer the question accurately and completely?

Does it

_____ identify the causes and effects?
_____ include a clear topic sentence?
_____ provide enough details to support the topic sentence?
_____ stay on the topic without including details that do not support the main idea?

Organization > Is the response clearly and logically organized?

Does it

_____ organize ideas so the answer is easy to understand?
_____ use transitional words that explain how the causes and effects are related?

Voice and Style > Does the response show skillful use of language?

Does it

_____ display vivid and precise word choices?
_____ use a tone appropriate to the topic and test situation?

Apply Your Skills ->

Read ->

Lewis and Clark Cross the Bitterroots

Before 1803, the United States occupied only the eastern half of North America. The country stopped at the Mississippi River. The land to the west was owned by France. President Thomas Jefferson wanted to gain control of that land and of the Mississippi River. In 1803, France offered to sell the land and Jefferson quickly bought it. It became known as the Louisiana Purchase.

Jefferson didn't know exactly what he was buying because little was known about the land west of the Mississippi. No one knew what was out there or even how big it was. In order to find out, Jefferson organized a group of explorers. He called them the Corps of Discovery and put Meriwether Lewis and William Clark in command.

In 1804, Lewis and Clark set out from St. Louis. The first part of the journey was by water. They traveled up the Missouri River as far as they could. Then they left the river and started cross-country. Soon, they reached what would be one of the hardest parts of their journey, crossing the Bitterroot Mountains in what is now Idaho and Montana.

It was September 11, 1805, when they started through the mountains. This was late in the year to cross the mountains since winter comes early to that region. Even without snow, this is a rugged area. There are many creeks to cross. Mountainsides are steep and rocky. Fallen trees and thick brush make walking difficult. Crossing this land was made worse by snow and cold weather.

To make matters worse, even before they entered the mountains, the expedition was low on food. And they found few deer or other animals to hunt. There was also little food for the horses. So at night, they wandered off in search of grass. In the morning, the men had to waste precious time finding their horses.

On September 14, the weather turned bad. The travelers endured rain, snow, and hail. They also lost time and energy when their guide lost the trail. When they camped, they were exhausted. Their hunters had found no food, so they were forced to kill a horse so they'd have something to eat.

The next day, the group found the trail again. They climbed steep mountainsides. Often the trail was on the edge of a drop-off. Any stumble could have been deadly. The group only made twelve miles that day. They needed to move faster before more bad weather caught them.

The next day, September 16, gave them a taste of how bad it could get. It started snowing before dawn and kept up all day. It was hard to follow the trail, such as it was. And as the group brushed against the trees, more snow fell on them. "I have been wet and as cold in every part as I ever was in my life," Clark wrote in his journal.

In the days that followed, the expedition stumbled on through the mountains. The horses were starving and weak. The explorers were as bad off. Several times, they had to kill a horse to have something to eat. But soon, they couldn't afford to kill more horses. They needed them to carry their supplies.

As the people and horses grew weaker and weaker, the journey became harder and they covered fewer miles. It was difficult to keep going, but they had no choice. Miserable as they were, they got up each day and struggled on. Finally, on September 22, the travelers reached the end of the Bitterroots. They had traveled 160 miles through some of the most rugged country in North America.

Jefferson purchased the land west of the Mississippi River for the United States. How did his action affect Lewis and Clark and their trip across the Bitterroots? Give five effects and explain how they are related to each other and to Jefferson's action.

Plan →

The following graphic organizer analyzes six causes and effects in the article. Complete the organizer.

Jefferson purchased the land west of the Mississippi.	→	Jefferson sent Lewis and Clark to explore the Louisiana Purchase.
Lewis and Clark crossed the Bitterroots in early winter.	→	They had to travel in rain, snow, and hail.
	→	

The following sentence describes the cause-and-effect relationship between the first two of the events. Write sentences to describe the next two events. Use transitional words to make the connections between causes and effects clear.

By the time Lewis and Clark reached the Bitterroots, it was already winter.

So they had to travel in rain, snow, and hail.

Practice: Write a topic sentence stating the main idea of your response to the question.

Topic sentence:

Write →

Jefferson purchased the land west of the Mississippi River for the United States. How did his action affect Lewis and Clark and their trip across the Bitterroots? Give five effects and explain how they are related to each other and to Jefferson's action.

Scoring Standards

Your answer will be scored based on the standards below. Review your writing. If it doesn't meet the standard, you won't receive the highest score. Revise to improve your response. If necessary, rewrite it on another piece of paper.

Content > Does the response answer the question accurately and completely?

Does it

_____ give five effects of Jefferson's action and explain how they are related?
_____ include a clear topic sentence?
_____ provide enough details to support the topic sentence?
_____ stay on the topic without including details that do not support the main idea?

Organization > Is the response clearly and logically organized?

Does it

_____ present ideas in an order that makes the answer easy to understand?
_____ include transitions to make the relationships among ideas clear?

Voice and Style > Does the response show skillful use of language?

Does it

_____ display vivid and precise word choices?
_____ use a variety of sentence structures, such as simple, compound, and complex sentences?
_____ use a tone appropriate to the topic and test situation?

Now, check your writing against the editing checklist below.

Mechanics

_____ capitalization
_____ punctuation
_____ spelling
_____ sentence fragments
_____ subject-verb agreement
_____ consistency of verb tenses
_____ paragraphing
_____ run-on sentences

Lesson 5:

Problem and Solution

Develop Your Skills ->

A **problem-and-solution** article tells about a problem. Then it tells about one or more solutions to the problem. Sometimes, the solutions give a satisfying answer to the problem. Other times, however, the solutions do not fully solve the problem.

To analyze a problem-and-solution article, first state the problem. Then create a chart like this one. Write each solution discussed in the article. Then write the results of the solution. These are the benefits or problems that result from the solution.

PROBLEM:	
SOLUTIONS	RESULTS
Solution 1	Result of solution 1
Solution 2	Result of solution 2
Solution 3	Result of solution 3

Read ->

FLATTENING THE EARTH

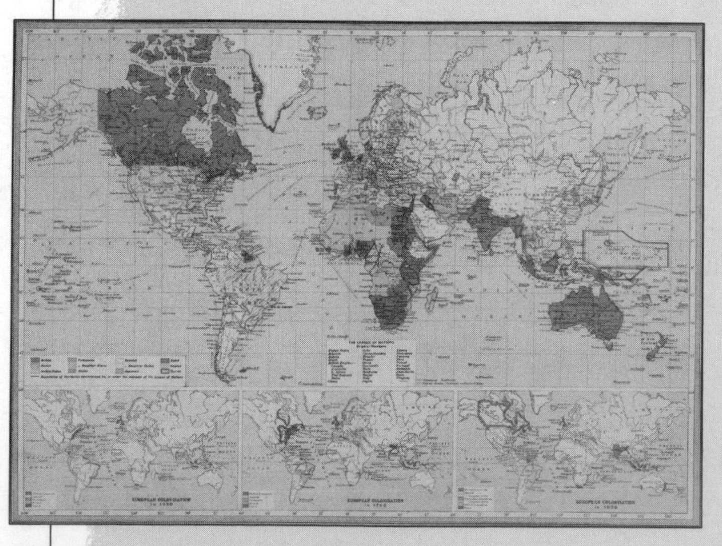

Mapmakers have long known that the earth is round like a ball. But they keep trying to make a flat map of it, and that's a problem.

Imagine that you're holding an orange. It represents a globe, which is a model of the earth. Now imagine peeling the orange. Cut the skin down one side and remove it whole. Try to lay the skin flat. It is impossible to spread the orange skin flat without tearing some parts of it. This is the problem that mapmakers have in trying to make a flat map of the round world.

Mapmakers have found different solutions to this problem. One way is to make several careful cuts from the top and bottom of the globe toward the center. Then the round surface will lie flat. And the countries and oceans are the correct sizes. The problem with this kind of world map is that it's hard to see how close one place is to another place because gaps are left where each cut is made.

Another solution is to stretch the top and bottom of the map so it will lie flat. This makes it easy to see directions. But it also creates distortions. It is impossible to tell how far apart cities are because the map has been stretched at the top and bottom. Also, some places look larger than they really are. For example, Greenland, which is an island near the top of the map, looks much larger than Africa, which is near the middle. That is because it is stretched more than Africa. Africa is actually more than fourteen times the size of Greenland.

Mapmakers have come up with other solutions, but each has problems. Of course the obvious solution is to leave the map round. That's a globe, and it shows the distances between places accurately. It also shows how large one island or country is relative to another island or country. But a globe is not a practical thing to take on a cross-country drive. It's too big and it doesn't pack easily.

So this is a problem without a perfect solution. The best we can do is to choose the solution that works best for the job we want to do. And then we must remember when looking at the map that it's not showing us exactly the way the earth really is.

What does the writer mean in saying there is no "perfect solution" to making a map of the earth? Give two examples from the passage to help explain your answer.

Plan →

Before you begin writing, create a chart to analyze the problem and solutions. Begin by stating the problem. Then list the possible solutions. Write the advantages and disadvantages of each.

Read the chart below. It analyzes Solution 1. Complete the chart by writing Solution 2 and the result of Solution 2.

PROBLEM: How can you make a flat map of the earth, which is round?	
SOLUTIONS	**RESULTS**
Make cuts at the top and bottom of the map. Creates gaps in the map so it can be spread flat.	Figuring out distances between places is difficult. Sizes of places on the map are accurate.

The following sentences describe the first solution and its results.

One solution makes cuts in the map. The places are the right size, but it's hard to judge distances because of the gaps.

Now write sentences describing the second solution and its results.

____

____

____

Look back at the question that follows the reading passage. Write a sentence that states the main idea of your answer. Use words from the prompt. This will be the topic sentence of your essay. This topic sentence has been written for you.

Topic sentence:

There is no perfect solution to making a map of the earth because the world is round, but maps are flat.

Write ->

Write your answer to the test question below. **What does the writer mean in saying there is no "perfect solution" to making a map of the earth? Give two examples from the passage to help explain your answer.** The answer has been started for you.

There is no perfect solution to making a map of the earth because the world is round, but maps are flat.

____

____

____

____

____

Review and Edit ->

Scoring Standards

Review and revise your writing based on the standards below. Then, check your answer for errors in spelling, grammar, and usage.

Content > Does the response answer the question accurately and completely?

Does it

_____ explain the problem?
_____ identify solutions described in the passage?
_____ include two examples to explain why the solutions are not perfect?
_____ include a clear topic sentence?
_____ stay on the topic without including details that do not support the main idea?

Organization > Is the response clearly and logically organized?

Does it

_____ organize ideas so the answer is easy to understand?
_____ include transitions to make the sequence of events clear?

Voice and Style > Does the response show skillful use of language?

Does it

_____ display vivid and precise word choices?
_____ use a tone appropriate to the topic and test situation?

Apply Your Skills

Read

Rabbit Wars

When people move to a new place, they often want to bring along things from home. They want to see familiar things. Sometimes, they bring animals and plants. Usually, this isn't a problem. But when people take them to a new land, big problems can arise. These newcomers sometimes take over the new land. They become pests and do great damage. And solutions are hard to find.

That was the case in Australia. In 1859, Thomas Austin wanted to hunt rabbits. So he set 24 rabbits free. And the rabbits did what rabbits do: they multiplied. Within a few years, they had become a plague. Few predators existed to keep them in check.

The rabbits were changing the land. They out-ate and out-bred native animals. They also took over the burrows used by other animals. So some native animals died out. Farms were overrun and crops were eaten. The rabbits ate grass that sheep and other farm animals needed. The land was overgrazed. Without the plants, the land eroded. Soil washed down rivers and blew away. Some native plants became extinct.

The farmers fought back. They used poisons and traps. Bounties were paid to hunters. But the rabbit problem grew. So the government began building a rabbit-proof fence. It would divide Australia. They wanted to keep the rabbits from taking over the whole continent. By 1903, the fence was 1138 miles long. It was the longest fence in the world. But it didn't work. The rabbits had spread beyond the fence before it was finished. By the 1940s, there were up to a billion rabbits.

All these efforts had little effect on the rabbits. But they hit native animals hard. These animals were sometimes poisoned or caught in traps meant for rabbits. Hunters hired to kill rabbits often killed native animals as well. Rabbits breed quickly, so they recovered from the attacks. But the native animals do not breed so quickly. They have never recovered from such great losses.

The loss of native plants and animals was a big problem. But people still thought the rabbits were the greatest threat. So in the 1950s, the government infected a few rabbits with a virus. Then they set them free. The sick rabbits spread the virus to other rabbits. About half a billion rabbits died. But the victory didn't last long. The rabbits that didn't die became immune to the virus. Within a few years, they were back.

In 1957 and 1966, the government attacked again. They set European rabbit fleas loose. They hoped the fleas would get the virus started again. It only worked for a short time. In 1993, the Spanish rabbit flea was set free. It died out in the Australian heat. In 1995, a new virus was set loose. It too only worked for a while. And so the rabbit wars go on.

People are fighting a problem they caused. Rabbits cost Australia about $600 million each year. They have changed the landscape forever. And unless they are controlled, more native mammals, insects, and plants will be lost.

What success have the Australians had in solving their rabbit problem? Give facts and examples from the article to support your response.

Plan ->

This chart analyzes the problems and solutions in the article. Complete the organizer.

PROBLEM: There are too many rabbits in Australia. They're causing changes to the land, causing the loss of native animals, and costing millions of dollars.	
SOLUTIONS	**RESULTS**
People tried to kill the rabbits with poisons and traps and by putting bounties on them.	Rabbits still increased in numbers. Native animals were often killed. Rabbits recovered, but native animals didn't.
Government built a long fence to contain the rabbits.	
The rabbits were infected with a virus.	

Write sentences describing the first solution and its results.

First they tried to kill them with poisons and traps and by setting bounties. Native animals were often killed instead. The rabbits recovered, but native animals didn't.

Now write sentences describing the second solution and its results.

Think about the question you will answer. Write a topic sentence that states the main idea of your answer to the essay question. You will use it as the topic sentence of your essay.

Topic sentence:

Write ->

Write your answer to the question. **What success have the Australians had in solving their rabbit problem? Give facts and examples from the article to support your response.**

Scoring Standards

Your answer will be scored based on the standards below. Review your writing. If it doesn't meet the standard, you won't receive the highest score. Revise to improve your response. If necessary, rewrite it on another piece of paper.

Content > Does the response answer the question accurately and completely?
Does it
_____ state the problem?
_____ describe the solutions?
_____ include a clear topic sentence?
_____ provide enough facts and examples to support the topic sentence?
_____ stay on the topic without including details that do not support the topic sentence?

Organization > Is the response clearly and logically organized?
Does it
_____ present ideas in an order that makes the answer easy to understand?
_____ include transitions to make the sequence of events clear?

Voice and Style > Does the response show skillful use of language?
Does it
_____ display vivid and precise word choices?
_____ use a variety of sentence structures, such as simple, compound, and complex sentences?
_____ use a tone appropriate to the topic and test situation?

Now, check your writing against the editing checklist below.

Mechanics

_____ capitalization
_____ punctuation
_____ spelling
_____ sentence fragments
_____ subject-verb agreement
_____ consistency of verb tenses
_____ paragraphing
_____ run-on sentences

Lesson 6: Fact and Opinion

Develop Your Skills –>

A **fact** is a statement, example, statistic, or observation. It can be proved to be true. An **opinion** is what somebody thinks or feels. An opinion may or may not be true. But it cannot be proved. In order to be taken seriously, opinions can be supported with facts and reasons.

Words such as *think, believe, suggest, probably,* or *maybe* often signal opinions. Statements of opinion often also include judgment words such as *great, fantastic, wonderful,* and *terrible.*

For help in analyzing facts and opinions in a passage, make a T-chart like this one. List details in the correct column as you read.

OPINIONS	FACTS SUPPORTING OPINIONS

Read –>

Pets and Our Health

Almost everyone likes dogs and cats. They're good for us too. But that's not just someone's opinion. Every day science is giving us more reasons to stay close to our pets. That's true whether we're healthy or sick.

For example, researchers have found that children with pets are more considerate than those without pets. Why? It's not certain. Perhaps it's because there are no surprises with animals. They don't deceive us. If an animal is unfriendly, you know it right away. If an animal needs help or attention, you know that too. Their body language is easy to read. And children learn that language quickly. In time, they learn to understand people better, too.

Here's a case study you might find interesting. Researchers have found that fish can help us get through a visit to the dentist. Watching fish helps reduce patient anxiety. Some dentists even keep dogs on hand to help calm patients.

Pets seem to help us regardless of our age. Studies show that elderly people who have pets make 16 percent fewer doctor visits than those who do not. Those who have dogs visit 21 percent less often.

In another study, Nancy Edwards, a nursing professor at Purdue University, studied 60 elderly patients in nursing homes. She brought in fish tanks. She said the patients seemed more relaxed and even more alert after watching the fish. And they ate 17.2 percent more food than before.

People with heart disease get important benefits from pets. Having pets around helps reduce blood pressure. Researchers at City Hospital in New York studied patients who had heart attacks. Those with pets were much more likely to survive the next year than those without pets.

It's not certain exactly why pets help us so much. One reason may be that pets accept us as we are. They don't judge us or care how popular we are. Some experts also say that pets help us get outside ourselves. People who are depressed or don't think highly of themselves think too much about themselves. Pets force us to think outside ourselves. We're no longer the center of the world. And that helps us relax.

So let's get close to our pets. Whether they're dogs, cats, fish, rabbits, or whatever, they have a way of helping us rclax and feel better.

At the beginning of the passage, the writer says that dogs and cats "are good for us." Identify three facts that support this statement of opinion.

Plan →

This T-chart collects and organizes information to answer the test question. The first column shows the writer's opinion. The second column lists facts from the passage that support the opinion. Review the passage and find more facts to support the opinion. Add two facts to the chart.

OPINION	FACTS SUPPORTING OPINIONS
Dogs and cats are good for us.	Elderly people who have pets make 16 percent fewer doctor visits than those who don't have pets.

Look at the diagram. The sample sentence below tells a fact that supports the opinion.

The writer points to elderly people who have pets around. They make 16 percent fewer doctor visits than those without pets.

Use the two facts you added to the chart. Tell how they support the writer's opinion.

Look back at the prompt that follows the reading passage. Write a sentence that states the main idea of your response. Use words from the prompt. This will be the topic sentence of your essay. This topic sentence has been written for you.

Topic sentence:

Many facts are given to support the writer's claim that dogs and cats "are good for us."

Write →

Write your response to the test prompt below. **At the beginning of the passage, the writer says that dogs and cats "are good for us." Identify three facts that support this statement of opinion.** The answer has been started for you. It begins with the topic sentence. Add two or three sentences of your own to complete the answer.

Many facts are given to support the writer's claim that dogs and cats "are good for us." The writer points to elderly people who have pets around.

____

____

____

____

____

Review and Edit →

Scoring Standards

Review and revise your writing based on the standards below. Then, check your answer for errors in spelling, grammar, and usage.

Content > Does the response answer the question accurately and completely?

Does it

_____ identify three facts that support the opinion?

_____ include a clear topic sentence?

_____ provide enough details to support the topic sentence?

_____ stay on the topic without including details that do not support the main idea?

Organization > Is the response clearly and logically organized?

Does it

_____ organize ideas so the answer is easy to understand?

Voice and Style > Does the response show skillful use of language?

Does it

_____ display vivid and precise word choices?

_____ use a tone appropriate to the topic and test situation?

Apply Your Skills ->

Read ->

A Town for the Deaf

Marvin T. Miller wants to build a town. That in itself is unusual. But what makes this town special is that American Sign Language (ASL) will be the official language. ASL is a language that uses hand signs. It is used by English-speaking people who are deaf and by those who want to talk with deaf persons.

Miller's new town, which will be called Laurent, will be built in South Dakota. ASL will be a daily part of the culture. Teachers will teach using ASL. Town council meetings will be held using ASL. Restaurants will be required to provide service using ASL. Laurent will be a place where people who use ASL will feel right at home. And that's the plan.

This all sounds like a great idea. But some people believe it's the wrong idea at the wrong time. Creating a town for deaf people, they claim, will isolate them. Children raised in Laurent will not know how to survive in the broader American culture. It is better, they say, for deaf people to join in the whole society.

But according to the Laurent web site, "Laurent is not a town built for deaf people. It is a town for people who use sign language." That does not mean everyone must be deaf or even use sign language. Anyone can live there. In fact, many of the residents will have normal hearing. Ninety percent of deaf children are born to parents with normal hearing. And many parents with one deaf child have other children with normal hearing. So, many of the townspeople will not be deaf. Laurent requires just one thing of people. They must accept ASL as a commonly used language.

Miller also takes issue with the claim that deaf people are better off living in society as a whole. Miller himself is deaf, and so are his wife and four children. "Society isn't doing that great a job of . . . integrating us," he points out. "My children don't see role models in their lives: mayors, factory managers, postal workers, business owners. So, we're setting up a place to show our unique culture, our unique society."

Critics claim, however, that sign language is dying. New medical breakthroughs are helping deaf people hear. Critics say that isolating the deaf in Laurent will only discourage them from making use of these new developments. But these solutions will not work for every deaf person. Plus, not everyone who is deaf wants them. Miller says he does not want them. Besides, he says, the "death of sign language and deaf culture continue to be greatly exaggerated." ASL is studied by more students in colleges today than all but four other languages.

Building a town for people who use sign language is unusual. It has not been tried before. So no one knows how it may turn out. The critics may be right. But Laurent offers the possibility of more fulfilling lives for deaf people. It is an experiment worth doing.

The writer claims that Laurent is an experiment worth doing. What facts and opinions are given to support this claim? Give at least three opinions and three facts.

Plan →

This T-chart collects and analyzes facts and opinions to answer the test question. Complete the chart.

OPINIONS	FACTS SUPPORTING OPINIONS
Society isn't doing a good job of integrating deaf people.	
Laurent won't isolate deaf people.	90% of deaf children have parents who can hear. Many deaf children have siblings who can hear.
	ASL is studied by more students in college than all but four other languages.

Identify the facts in your chart.

ASL is studied by more students in college than all but four other languages.

Practice: Write a topic sentence stating the main idea of your response to the question.

Topic sentence:

Write →

Write your answer to the question. **The writer claims that Laurent is an experiment worth doing. What facts and opinions are given to support this claim? Give at least three opinions and two facts.**

Review and Edit ->

Scoring Standards

Your answer will be scored based on the standards below. Review your writing. If it doesn't meet the standard, you won't receive the highest score. Revise to improve your response. If necessary, rewrite it on another piece of paper.

Content > Does the response answer the question accurately and completely?

Does it

______ identify at least two facts?
______ identify at least three opinions?
______ include a clear topic sentence?
______ provide enough details to support the topic sentence?
______ stay on the topic without including details that do not support the topic sentence?

Organization > Is the response clearly and logically organized?

Does it

______ present ideas in an order that makes the answer easy to understand?

Voice and Style > Does the response show skillful use of language?

Does it

______ display vivid and precise word choices?
______ use a variety of sentence structures, such as simple, compound, and complex sentences?
______ use a tone appropriate to the topic and test situation?

Now, check your writing against the editing checklist below.

Mechanics

______ capitalization
______ punctuation
______ spelling
______ sentence fragments
______ subject-verb agreement
______ consistency of verb tenses
______ paragraphing
______ run-on sentences

The Shot Heard Round the World

It shouldn't have surprised anyone when the fighting started. Massachusetts had been the scene of heated debate and angry words for months. People were talking about war. A few colonists—firebrands like John Hancock and Samuel Adams—even called for independence. And some people were getting ready to fight for it. They were gathering guns and ammunition. They put them aside to field an army, should it go that far.

It was 1775. The colonies in America were restless under the rule of Great Britain. They didn't like the taxes laid on them. And they didn't like watching the British troops march in their streets or live in their homes. They didn't like the British government in faraway London telling them what to do and never asking what they thought. The British weren't happy with matters either. It was a dangerous time in the colonies. The situation was tense. The smallest incident might spark war.

So the British decided to reduce the risk. British General Thomas Gage was sent to capture weapons stored in Concord. Without their weapons, the threat of war would be cut. Concord was a town about 15 miles from Boston. Gage was also supposed to arrest Hancock and Adams. The two rebel leaders were staying in the nearby town of Lexington. Gage was a veteran soldier. He didn't want to stir up the colonists. So he tried to keep his plan secret. He ordered his troops to move at night. The British force was made up of about 700 soldiers.

The colonists, however, knew something was about to happen. So they kept a watch on Gage and his army. When they saw the troops begin to move they sent word to Paul Revere and William Dawes. These two men raced ahead of the British troops. They rode through the night to warn Hancock, Adams, and the other patriots. They knew the British would be patrolling the roads, looking for anyone who might try to warn the rebels. As a result, Revere and Dawes followed separate routes. In case one was captured, the other might get through. As they rode, they warned colonists along the way.

Remember the steps:

Read
Plan
Write
Review & Edit

Revere and Dawes met at Lexington. There they also met up with Dr. Samuel Prescott. Then the three of them rode on toward Concord. On the way, Revere and Dawes were caught by the British. Prescott, however, escaped and continued the mission. Meanwhile, church bells were being rung, rifles fired, and drums beaten to alert people in the countryside. The British were coming.

When an advance party of about 250 British troops reached Lexington, they were met by an American militia of about 70 soldiers. A militia is an army. It's made up of civilians who come together during times of crisis. The militiamen were commanded by Captain John Parker. The British were under the command of Major John Pitcairn.

Pitcairn knew he had the advantage. He had more troops, and they were better trained and equipped. Plus, he knew a large force of British troops was right behind him. He called out to the militiamen to give up. At the same time, he ordered his troops to surround the militia and disarm them. Parker realized that the odds were against him. He ordered his troops to break up and leave rather than be captured. Just as they started to leave, a single shot rang out. To this day, no one knows who fired it. But this shot signaled the beginning of the American Revolution.

The British thought the rebels had fired the shot. So they returned fire. Eight of the Americans were killed and ten wounded. The rest of the militia retreated and hid in the woods.

The British won this first small victory. This wasn't the end of the day, though. As a smaller force of about 150 British soldiers marched on to Concord, the patriots were gathering. By the time the British got to Concord, 400 patriots stood before them. This time there was less hesitation; both sides exchanged shots. And this time, it was the British who broke and ran.

The British retreated all the way to Boston. Seven hundred of them had left Boston the night before. But more and more patriots were gathering. Before long, 5,000 of them accompanied the British on their retreat. They shot at them from behind trees and rock walls and then ran away to avoid a pitched battle. The British weren't used to fighting this way and paid dearly for it. They lost about 73 soldiers on the retreat to Boston.

The greatest effect of the battles at Lexington and Concord was the war they started. The American Revolution had begun, and more colonists joined the cause of independence. By the end of the war, the new American nation was born.

1. **How did the actions of British troops affect Paul Revere and William Dawes? Identify and explain three effects.**

2. **Would events have developed differently if Revere, Dawes, and Prescott had not been involved? Explain at least two ways that events might have changed.**

3. In 1775, many American colonists were growing unhappy with British rule. Some leaders began to talk of rebellion. Explain the chain of events that led from this situation to the fighting at Lexington and Concord. Identify and explain five events.

____

____

____

____

____

____

____

____

____

____

____

____

____

____

Checklist

Content, Organization, and Style

_____ Accurate, complete response
_____ Causes and effects
_____ Events clearly related
_____ Topic sentence
_____ Supporting details
_____ Logical organization
_____ Transitional words
_____ Vivid, precise word choices
_____ Appropriate tone

Spelling, Grammar, and Usage

_____ Capitalization
_____ Punctuation
_____ Spelling
_____ Fragments and run-on sentences
_____ Subject and verb agreement
_____ Consistent verb tenses
_____ Correct paragraphs

Over the Chilkoot and Down the Yukon

In July 1897, two ships docked in San Francisco and Seattle. They carried gold that had been discovered in the Yukon Territories in Canada. News spread rapidly. Within weeks thousands of gold-hunters were heading for the Yukon. Within six months, 100,000 men and women were on their way. They were called stampeders because they were rushing, or stampeding, to the gold fields.

Most took a ship to Alaska. That was the easy part. Then they went overland. Most stampeders would climb Chilkoot Pass. Then they would travel north through a series of lakes to the Yukon River. From there, they followed the river to Dawson City and the gold fields along the Klondike River.

Travel was dangerous and difficult. And no matter when they traveled, every season had challenges. During fall and winter, they faced ice, snow, and terrible cold. In the spring and summer, they struggled through mud and flooding rivers and streams. But the stampeders didn't pick their season for travel. They raced to the Klondike as fast as possible while there was still gold to be found. The journey was incredibly rugged and dangerous.

Carrying food and supplies added to the difficulties of the journey. Little food and few supplies were available in the Yukon. The Northwest Mounted Police didn't want stampeders going into the territory unprepared. It was a remote and isolated region. It had severe winter weather. And there would be little help for the stampeders if they got into trouble. So the Mounties demanded that everyone bring plenty of supplies with them. The Mounties refused to let stampeders enter the country unless each one carried about a ton of food and supplies.

Climbing over Chilkoot pass was probably the most difficult part of the journey. The last part of it was called the Golden Stairs. This steep section rose 1,000 feet in the final one-half mile. It was covered in ice and was too steep for pack animals. So the stampeders had to haul their supplies up the mountain on their backs. To make it possible to climb to the pass, 1,500 steps were carved out of the ice. Even with the help of the steps, this was no easy route. The stampeders loaded 50 or 60 pounds of supplies on their backs and climbed. Climbing to the top would take about six hours. Then they had to go back down, get another load, and haul it up.

Going back down was easier than climbing up. Stampeders took the fast route, a series of slides. These were carved out of the ice beside the stairs. It only took a few moments to reach the bottom.

When stampeders reached the top of Chilkoot Pass, they headed north to the Yukon River. The first leg took them 30 miles to Lake Bennett. The route was primitive. The stampeders waded through marshes. They cut down trees to bridge dangerous streams. They walked along the edges of steep drop-offs. All the while, they carried their ton of supplies. They would trudge four or five miles and leave their 60-pound load. Then they would go back, and pick up another load and haul it forward. They went back and forth over the same route until they got all their supplies together. Then they set out on the next five miles.

After reaching Bennett Lake, the route to the Klondike followed the Yukon River. Those who reached Bennett Lake in the early spring had a choice to make. They could go ahead, traveling over the frozen river. But they had to travel fast. Otherwise, the ice would become thin and begin breaking up. Then they would be stranded. Their other choice was to wait for the thaw. Then they could build boats and travel by water. Those who chose to travel by water made the 500-mile trip to Dawson City in about three weeks.

But there was a problem with this choice too. The boats were always overloaded. And many stampeders knew little about boats. Some were so badly built that they sank within a few miles. The river was mostly easy traveling. But near the present day city of Whitehorse, terrible rapids broke up the river. During the first days of the gold rush, more than 100 boats were lost there. The rapids were so dangerous that the Northwest Mounted Police set rules. No boats could go through without an experienced pilot. Once through the Whitehorse rapids, the Yukon became gentler. There were some smaller rapids. But most stampeders got through them safely.

After the long trek through the wilderness, Dawson City would have been a welcome sight. But stampeders found little gold waiting for them. Most mining claims had been taken by locals long before the first stampeders arrived.

1. The matter of food and supplies created a problem for both the Mounted Police and the stampeders. Explain the problem and how the Mounted Police solved it.

____

____

____

____

____

____

____

____

2. What problems did the stampeders face in crossing Chilkoot pass? Explain the problems and the solution.

____

____

____

____

____

____

____

____

3. Stampeders who reached the Yukon River early in the spring had a choice to make. Each choice had different problems and solutions. What were the problems and the solutions?

____

____

____

____

____

____

____

____

____

____

____

____

____

____

Checklist

Content, Organization, and Style

______ Accurate, complete response
______ Problem explained
______ Solutions described
______ Topic sentence
______ Supporting details
______ Logical organization
______ Transitional words
______ Vivid, precise word choices
______ Appropriate tone

Spelling, Grammar, and Usage

______ Capitalization
______ Punctuation
______ Spelling
______ Fragments and run-on sentences
______ Subject and verb agreement
______ Consistent verb tenses
______ Correct paragraphs

Dying Tongues

Language is part of our daily lives. It connects us to our friends and family. It connects us to the world. It helps us think about things that are important to us. It allows us to say how we feel. It permits us to name an object and to call our dog. What would we do if our language disappeared?

Hard as it is to imagine, languages are disappearing around the world. Linguists say that on average a language dies every two weeks. Linguists are people who study language.

You only have to look at Native American languages to see what is happening. When Columbus reached America, there were about 300 languages spoken in North America. Today, there are about half that number. Linguists think that by 2050, only about 20 of these languages will remain.

Linguists think that there are about 6,800 living languages in the world. Living languages are those that are spoken by people on a daily basis. That sounds like a lot of languages. But 90 percent of them are spoken by fewer than 100,000 people. About 350 are spoken by fewer than 50 people. And 46 have just one living, native speaker.

On the other hand, about 250 languages are spoken by at least a million people. Mandarin Chinese, English, and Spanish are the most widely spoken languages. And they are squeezing out all those other tongues.

It's natural for languages to develop, change, spread, and fade away. But what is happening is not following the natural cycle. Local politics, global business, and social pressure are affecting languages. For example, in East Africa, Swahili is the most important language. It is the main tongue used for business. It is used on TV and radio. It is used by political leaders. Speakers of less common languages are shut out. They find it hard to succeed. They can't listen to the news or sports. They can't share in the political life of the country. So, many people learn Swahili. Little by little, the first tongue becomes weaker. It is spoken less often by fewer people. Finally it will die. And only Swahili will remain.

These same pressures are affecting languages throughout the world. But many people want to save these disappearing languages. Why? If they have no purpose, why should we care about them? Isn't the purpose of language so people can talk to one another? Wouldn't it be better to have fewer languages? More people could talk to each other more easily.

Many people think the answer is *no.* All of the world's many languages are important. Each tongue holds part of our human culture and history. People in a certain place created it to meet specific, local conditions. A language tells about the people who created it. The Yeli Dnye language of New Guinea, for example, has an unusual vocabulary for describing colors. Several languages in East Africa are spoken with clicks. No other language in the world uses clicks. Why is this? These are important matters. They help us know our history. They help us know who we are, and why.

Language is not just a collection of words. It holds specialized information. It is the glue that holds a culture together. If we lose a language, we may lose much of the knowledge held by a culture. For example, people in northern Australia were once infected by a serious skin disease. Doctors couldn't find a cure. But native people told a nurse about a cure from a local plant. She tried it, and it worked. If the native tongue had disappeared, knowledge of this plant might have been lost as well.

Some people believe their native tongues are sacred. They are the means to talk about their faith. English or another language cannot replace these first languages. They do not have the same words and cannot express the same feelings.

Languages are also a source of independence. A language holds the members of a society together. It is something they share. It sets them apart from outsiders. It unites them.

Some people say that it is good if people merge into one society. There will be less conflict, fewer wars. That may be true. But it is also true that the richness of society will be lost. There will be fewer people with different ideas. There will be fewer points of view. Will people begin thinking too much alike? Will we lose some of our creativity as humans? Will we have fewer solutions to the problems that will arise in the future? There may not be answers to these questions today. But what if the answer is *yes?* Once the languages are gone, it will be too late to recover them. Our human society will forever be without the wisdom and insights that these languages held for us.

1. The writer states that languages are disappearing around the world. What are three facts that support this opinion?

____

____

____

____

____

____

____

____

2. The writer says that languages that are disappearing today are not following the natural cycle. What are three facts the writer gives to support that opinion?

____

____

____

____

____

____

____

____

3. The writer says that all the world's languages are important. Give three opinions and two facts to support this idea.

____

____

____

____

____

____

____

____

____

____

____

____

____

____

Checklist

Content, Organization, and Style

_____ Accurate, complete response
_____ Facts identified
_____ Opinions identified
_____ Topic sentence
_____ Supporting details
_____ Logical organization
_____ Transitional words
_____ Vivid, precise word choices
_____ Appropriate tone

Spelling, Grammar, and Usage

_____ Capitalization
_____ Punctuation
_____ Spelling
_____ Fragments and run-on sentences
_____ Subject and verb agreement
_____ Consistent verb tenses
_____ Correct paragraphs

Lesson 7: Comparison and Contrast

Develop Your Skills →

Comparison-and-contrast writing tells how two or more subjects are similar and different. Comparing means to identify ways in which subjects are alike. Contrasting means to identify ways in which they are different.

Writers often use transitional words such as *like, also,* and *in the same way* to signal comparisons. They often use words such as *but, however,* and *on the contrary* to signal contrasts. But they may simply give the details and expect the reader to figure out the similarities and differences. Use a Venn diagram to record these similarities and differences.

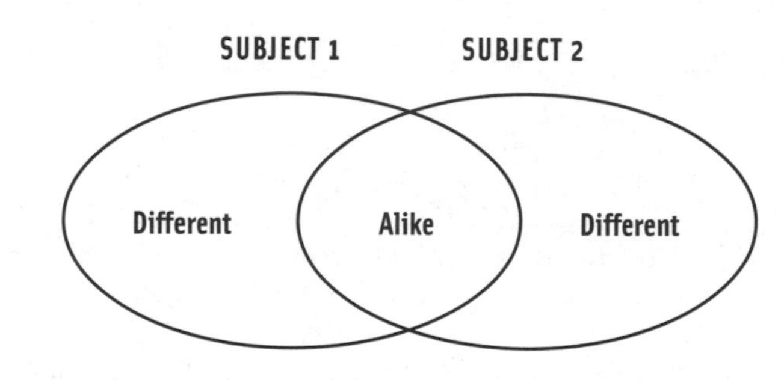

The Two Faces of Lewis Carroll

You know Lewis Carroll as the man who wrote *Alice's Adventures in Wonderland* and *Through the Looking Glass*. You may not know him as Charles Lutwidge Dodgson. That's the name his parents gave him. It's also the name he used every day. He chose the name Lewis Carroll for writing.

Dodgson was born in England in 1832. Even as a child, he had an interest in math and puzzles. He also had a strong sense of humor. When he was twenty-nine, he became a deacon in the Church of England. He then continued his studies in mathematics and logic. In time, he became a teacher at Oxford University. He never much liked teaching, however. He was bored by his students. They didn't want to learn what he had to teach. But he did care about math. He wrote about 30 dense works on math and logic. Some were textbooks. Others were studies meant for scholars. His writings were useful and practical but not brilliant. They were certainly not entertaining. Though the books were well received at the time, no one reads them anymore. He published these works under the name of Dodgson.

There was another side to Dodgson, however. It was his creative side. At fourteen, he began writing small magazines for his brothers and sisters. They were made up of drawings, stories, and poems. Later, he wanted to become an artist. He soon realized he didn't have the skill to be a good one. So he gave up on this dream. But he enjoyed art his whole life.

Little by little, Dodgson turned toward writing. He published *Alice's Adventures in Wonderland* in 1865. In it, he expressed a side of himself that had been hidden beneath his academic studies.

Alice's Adventures in Wonderland was very successful. Dodgson followed it up with *Through the Looking Glass.* It was also a success. These were both published under the name of Lewis Carroll. These and most of Carroll's literary works are rich in fantasy and nonsense. These features create a sense of childhood and freedom. Carroll had a deep, creative imagination.

Dodgson died in 1898. Today, Lewis Carroll is remembered for his imaginative stories of Alice in Wonderland and for a few poems. These writings are still popular today. Charles Dodgson was successful in his own way. However, today his work in math is almost entirely forgotten. Few people even know Dodgson and Carroll are the same person.

In an essay, compare and contrast the works of Charles Dodgson and Lewis Carroll. Identify at least one way in which they are alike and at least two ways in which they are different.

Plan →

This Venn diagram shows how the works of Dodgson and Carroll are alike and different. Review the passage. Find one way in which they are alike and another way in which they are different. Complete the diagram.

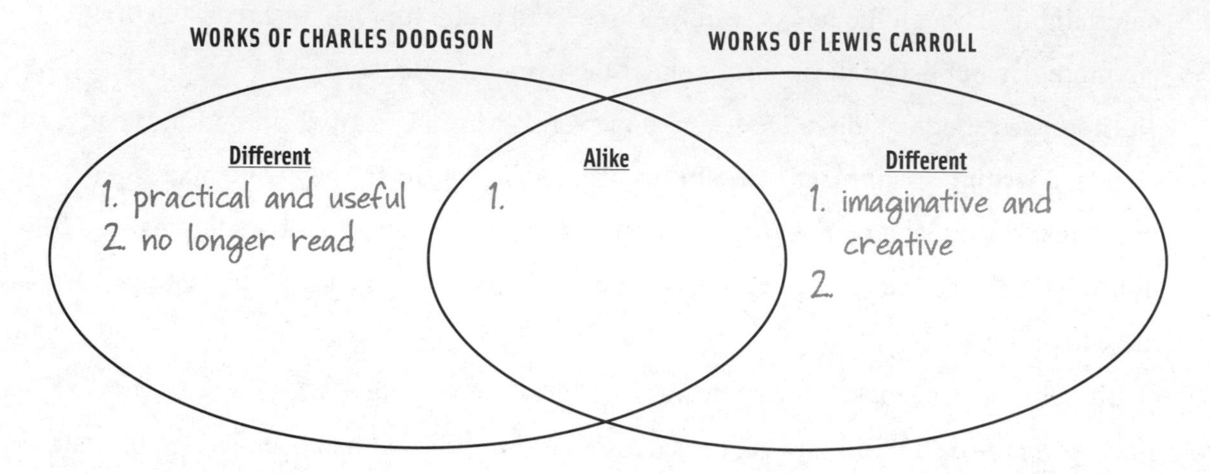

The model sentence contrasts two of the details from the diagram.

While Dodgson's works in mathematics and logic were practical and useful, Carroll's writings were imaginative and creative.

Write one or two sentences showing how two more details are different.

____

____

____

Look back at the prompt that follows the reading passage. Write a sentence that states the main idea of your response. Use words from the prompt. This will be the topic sentence of your essay.

Topic sentence:

The works of Charles Dodgson and Lewis Carroll are both similar and different.

Write →

Write your response to the test prompt below. **In an essay, compare and contrast the works of Charles Dodgson and Lewis Carroll. Identify at least one way in which they are alike and at least two ways in which they are different.** The answer has been started for you. It begins with the topic sentence. Complete the essay.

The works of Charles Dodgson and Lewis Carroll are both similar and different. While Dodgson's work in mathematics and logic were practical and useful, Carroll's writings were imaginative and creative.

____

____

____

____

Review and Edit →

Scoring Standards

Review and revise your writing based on the standards below. Then, check your answer for errors in spelling, grammar, and usage.

Content > Does the response answer the question accurately and completely?

Does it

_____ state one way in which the works are alike?
_____ state two ways in which the works are different?
_____ include a clear topic sentence?
_____ use examples or other details to support your ideas?
_____ stay on the topic without including details that do not support the main idea?

Organization > Is the response clearly and logically organized?

Does it

_____ organize ideas so the answer is easy to understand?

Voice and Style > Does the response show skillful use of language?

Does it

_____ display vivid and precise word choices?
_____ use a tone appropriate to the topic and test situation?

Apply Your Skills →

Read →

Harry Potter: The Boy Next Door

The Harry Potter books have been an amazing success. Millions of people around the world have read the books. Moreover, they're not just books for younger readers. Adults devour the books, too. What accounts for this incredible popularity? There are probably many answers. To begin with, they're good books with strong plots and lots of action. It's not always easy to tell who the bad guys are, but you know that evil is lurking. And there stands young Harry Potter, ready to battle evil to the bitter end. You can't help rooting for him.

One of the strongest explanations for the success of the novels, however, is the ordinariness of the character of Harry Potter. Ordinary, you say? What's ordinary about Harry? He's a wizard and the son of famous wizards, and he goes to wizard school and is surrounded by wizards. He fights dragons and evil magicians and the powerful forces of evil. There's nothing ordinary about that!

But look more closely at this character. Harry's a regular kid. In fact, you might even say he's a bit of a nerd. You'll never confuse him with the street-smart, hip kids that you usually see on TV and starring in movies. Harry's not fashionable and he sure doesn't talk or walk like most of those confident, enviable teen stars. On the contrary, he wants to be normal. He's quiet and has a strong moral streak. He likes sports and is surprisingly good at them. When he plays Quidditch in *Harry Potter and the Sorcerer's Stone,* he has the help of a special model of the Firebolt. But he wins on smarts and skill too.

Of course, Harry's not perfect. He tends to put off his studies, and he doesn't read nearly enough. He doesn't always make wise decisions and sometimes his anger gets the best of him. For example, living with his stepparents, the Dursleys, is a trial. One day, in a fit of frustration, his simmering rage boils over. He turns his magic on Aunt Marge, blowing her up like a balloon. Then he grabs his wand and aims it at Uncle Vernon before racing from the house.

Like any teenager, Harry sometimes feels misunderstood and mistreated. In *Order of the Phoenix,* everyone, it seems, thinks Harry is a liar who's only out to get attention. Of course,

Harry doesn't see himself that way, and he's hurt by the misunderstanding.

Harry's brave and loyal, too. He knows who his friends are, and he stands by them and tries to protect them. In *Harry Potter and the Sorcerer's Stone,* Harry goes off on a dangerous mission in search of the Sorcerer's Stone. He tries to convince Ron and Hermione to stay behind. He doesn't want them to risk their lives. And while Harry often shows bravery, his courage sometimes fails him. In his fourth year, he falls in love with Cho Chang. He wants in the worst way to ask her to the Yule Ball. Just a week before, he had faced the Hungarian Horntail dragon—an act of great courage. But when it comes to asking Cho to the ball, he's overcome with cowardice.

Looking at Harry's personality like this, who does he remind you of? Look closely, and honestly. It might be you or many of your friends. He's just an ordinary kid, doing the best he can. Not surprisingly, most readers identify with this ordinary kid. They see themselves in Harry, and they root for him to win. It's easy to see why they can't put the books down once they start reading.

Compare and contrast Harry Potter to an ordinary kid. Give two details that show how he's different and five details that show how he's ordinary. Include at least two examples to support your answer.

Plan →

This Venn diagram compares and contrasts details about Harry Potter from the passage. Complete the diagram.

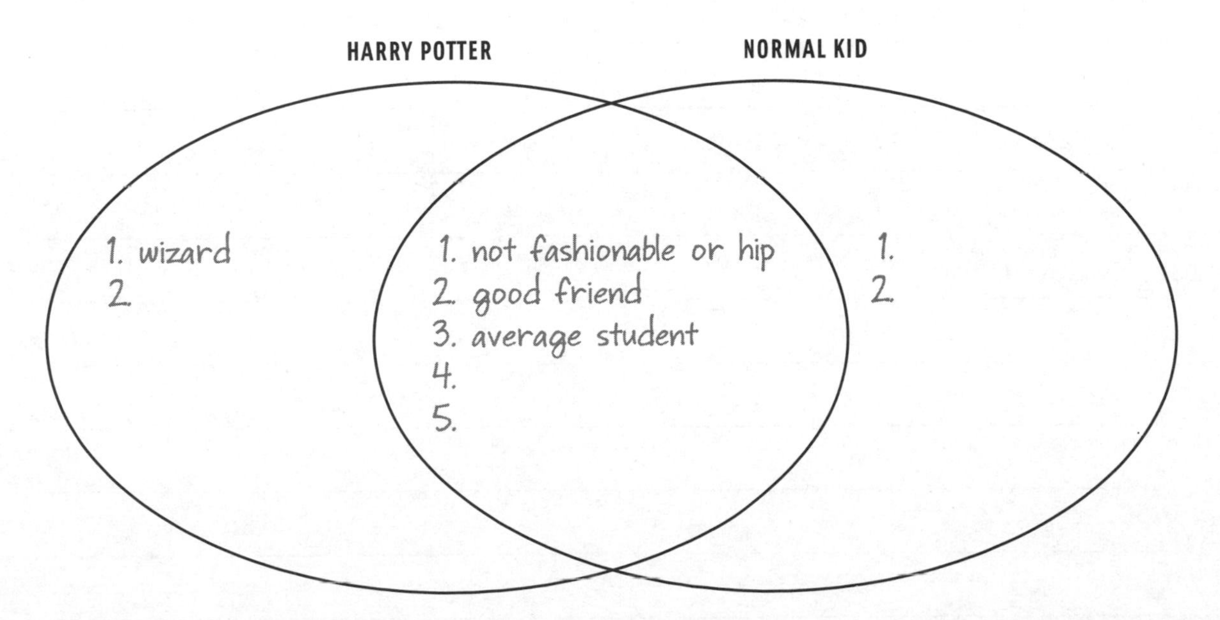

Write two or three sentences. Explain how two of the details show that Harry is an ordinary person. Give an example of one detail.

Write a topic sentence stating the main idea of your response to the prompt.

Topic sentence:

Although Harry Potter is not an ordinary person, he is like one in many ways.

Write →

Compare and contrast Harry Potter to an ordinary kid. Give two details that show how he's different and five details that show how he's ordinary. Include at least two examples to support your answer.

Review and Edit ->

Scoring Standards

Your answer will be scored based on the standards below. Review your writing. If it doesn't meet the standard, you won't receive the highest score. Revise to improve your response. If necessary, rewrite it on another piece of paper.

Content > Does the response answer the question accurately and completely?

Does it

_____ state two ways in which Harry is different from ordinary people?
_____ state five ways in which Harry is like ordinary people?
_____ include at least two examples to support your ideas?
_____ include a clear topic sentence?
_____ stay on the topic without including details that do not support the main idea?

Organization > Is the response clearly and logically organized?

Does it

_____ present ideas in an order that makes the answer easy to understand?
_____ include transitions to make the relationships among ideas clear?

Voice and Style > Does the response show skillful use of language?

Does it

_____ display vivid and precise word choices?
_____ use a variety of sentence structures, such as simple, compound, and complex sentences?
_____ use a tone appropriate to the topic and test situation?

Now, check your writing against the editing checklist below.

Mechanics

_____ capitalization
_____ punctuation
_____ spelling
_____ sentence fragments
_____ subject-verb agreement
_____ consistency of verb tenses
_____ paragraphing
_____ run-on sentences

Lesson 8: Plot

Develop Your Skills ->

The **plot** of a story is the events that move the story forward. Plot is made up of these five parts:

Exposition—This part introduces the characters, setting, and situation.
Rising Action—Events introduce and develop a conflict. Suspense builds as the conflict becomes more intense.
Climax—The suspense reaches its highest point and a solution becomes clear.
Falling Action—These events lead to a solution.
Resolution—The conflict ends and loose ends are wrapped up. The climax, falling action, and resolution occur so close to the end that these parts happen together.

For help in analyzing the plot of a short story, create a simple plot diagram. List events and other elements of the story.

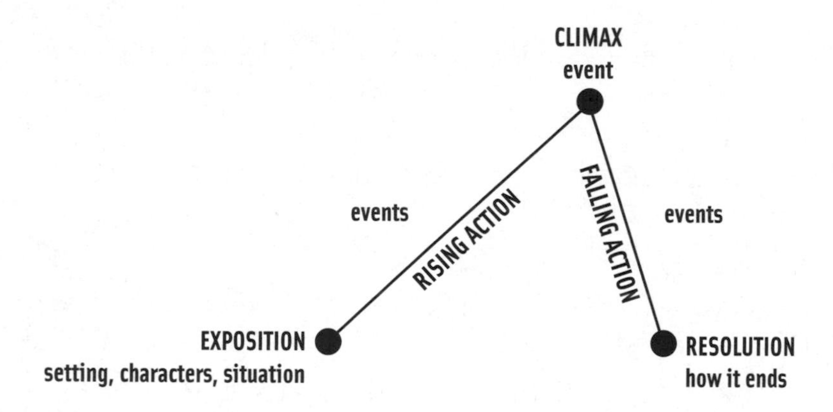

Read ->

Cherokee Myth of the Pleiades

The Cherokee are a group of American Indians who once lived in what is now the southeastern United States. Now, most of them live in Oklahoma. The Cherokee are an ancient people with many myths that tell how things of this world came into being. Here is a tale about a group of stars called the Pleiades.

When the earth was new, seven Cherokee boys spent all their time playing a game called gatayu'sti down by the townhouse. A disk-shaped stone was rolled along the ground. The boys would strike at it with a stick. They were so absorbed in their play that they did not do their chores and help their families raise corn for food. Their mothers scolded them, but the boys paid no attention.

So one day, the mothers decided to teach their sons a lesson. They collected gatayu'sti stones and put them with the corn in the dinner pot. Then they served the boys stones with their corn, and when the boys complained, the mothers responded, "Because you like your game of gatayu'sti so well that you neglect your family, now you can eat your gatayu'sti."

The boys were angry and rushed off and began dancing furiously in a circle around the townhouse. They danced faster and faster, all the while complaining about how their mothers had treated them and praying to the spirits for help.

Their mothers, meanwhile, began to feel guilty, so they went to the townhouse to make up with their sons. When they arrived, the boys were still dancing their wild circle dance. But something more was happening; they were rising slowly into the air. With each circle, they rose higher. The mothers rushed to their sons to pull them back to earth, but all the boys except one were too high to reach. Slowly they ascended farther and farther into the sky until they reached the heavens. There they became a group of stars the Cherokee call Ani'tsutsa, which means "The Boys." Those stars are still there. Most people today call them the Pleiades.

The one boy who was caught by his mother came crashing down so hard he fell into the earth, disappearing from sight. But soon, a green plant grew where he had disappeared. The plant grew larger and became a pine tree. And the vast pine forests of the mountains grew from that first tree.

Which event is the climax of the story? How do you know? Give four details from the story to support your answer.

Plan →

This diagram organizes information needed to answer the test question. It shows the exposition and the events that make up the climax and falling action. Add two events that are part of the rising action. Add the resolution.

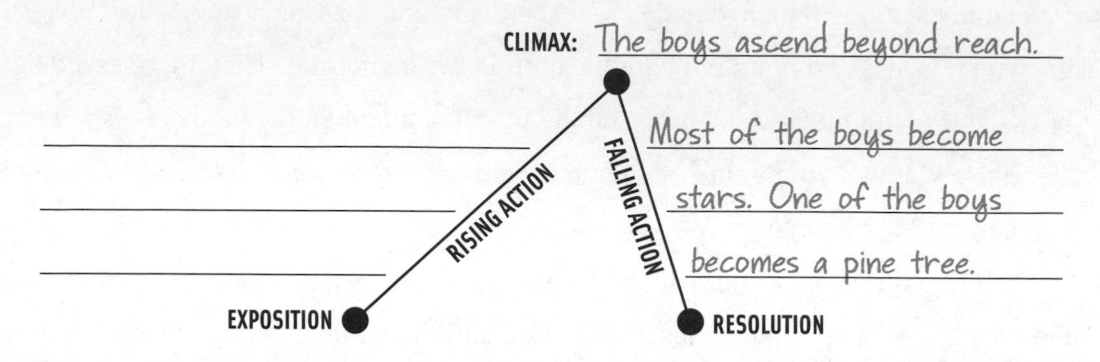

The model sentences explain that the suspense lessens following the climax and gives two events that support the statement.

After the climax, the suspense lessens as the writer tells what happens. Most of the boys become stars and one becomes a pine tree.

Now, write one or two sentences telling how the events you added to the diagram help build the suspense.

Look back at the question that follows the reading passage. Write a sentence that states the main idea of your answer. Use words from the prompt. This will be the topic sentence of your essay. This topic sentence has been written for you.

Topic sentence:

The climax occurs when the mothers rush to save their sons who have by then ascended beyond their reach.

Write ->

Write your answer to the test question below. **Which event is the climax? How do you know when the climax occurs? Give four details from the story to support your response.** The answer has been started for you. It begins with the topic sentence.

The climax occurs when the mothers rush to save their sons who have by then ascended beyond their reach.

Review and Edit ->

Scoring Standards

Review and revise your writing based on the standards below. Then, check your answer for errors in spelling, grammar, and usage.

Content > Does the response answer the question accurately and completely?

Does it

_____ describe the climax of the story?
_____ tell how you know when the climax occurs?
_____ give four details to support the answer?
_____ include a clear topic sentence?
_____ stay on the topic without including details that do not support the main idea?

Organization > Is the response clearly and logically organized?

Does it

_____ organize ideas so the answer is easy to understand?
_____ include transitions to make the sequence of events clear?

Voice and Style > Does the response show skillful use of language?

Does it

_____ display vivid and precise word choices?
_____ use a tone appropriate to the topic and test situation?

Apply Your Skills →

Read →

"A Detail"

by Stephen Crane

The tiny old lady in the black dress and curious little black bonnet had at first seemed alarmed at the sound made by her feet upon the stone pavements. But later she forgot about it, for she suddenly came into the tempest of the Sixth Avenue shopping district, where from the streams of people and vehicles went up a roar like that from headlong mountain torrents.

She seemed then like a chip that catches, recoils, turns, and wheels, a reluctant thing in the clutch of the impetuous river. She hesitated, faltered, debated with herself. Frequently she seemed about to address people; then all of a sudden she would evidently lose her courage. Meanwhile the torrent jostled her, swung her this way and that way.

At last, however, she saw two young women gazing in at a shop window. They were well-dressed girls; they wore gowns with enormous sleeves that made them look like full-rigged ships with all sails set. They seemed to have plenty of time; they leisurely scanned the goods in the window. Other people had made the tiny old woman much afraid because obviously they were speeding to keep such tremendously important engagements. She went close to the girls and peered in at the same window. She watched them furtively for a time. Then finally she said: "Excuse me!"

The girls looked down at this old face with its two large eyes turned toward them.

"Excuse me: can you tell me where I can get any work?"

For an instant the two girls stared. Then they seemed about to exchange a smile, but, at the last moment, they checked it. The tiny old lady's eyes were upon them. She was quaintly serious, silently expectant. She made one marvel that in that face the wrinkles showed no trace of experience, knowledge; they were simply little soft, innocent creases. As for her glance, it had the trustfulness of ignorance and the candor of babyhood.

"I want to get something to do, because I need the money," she continued, since, in their astonishment, they had not replied to her first question. "Of course I'm not strong and I couldn't do very much, but I can sew well; and in a house where there was a good many menfolks, I could do all the mending. Do you know of any place where they would like me to come?"

The young women did then exchange a smile, but it was a subtle tender smile, the edge of personal grief.

"Well, no, madam," hesitatingly said one of them at last; "I don't think I know anyone."

A shade passed over the tiny old lady's face, a shadow of the wing of disappointment. "Don't you?" she said, with a little struggle to be brave in her voice.

Then the girl hastily continued: "But if you will give me your address, I may find someone, and if I do, I will surely let you know of it."

The tiny old lady dictated her address, bending over to watch the girl write on a visiting card with a silver pencil. Then she said: "I thank you very much." She bowed to them, smiling, and went on down the avenue.

As for the two girls, they walked to the curb and watched this aged figure, small and frail, in its black gown and curious black bonnet. At last, the crowd, the innumerable wagons, intermingling and changing with uproar and riot, suddenly engulfed it.

Explain how the suspense builds up to the climax of "A Detail." Support your answer by identifying the climax and three events in the rising action.

Plan →

This graphic organizer identifies events that lead to the climax of the story. Complete the chart by listing another event in the rising action and the event that marks the climax.

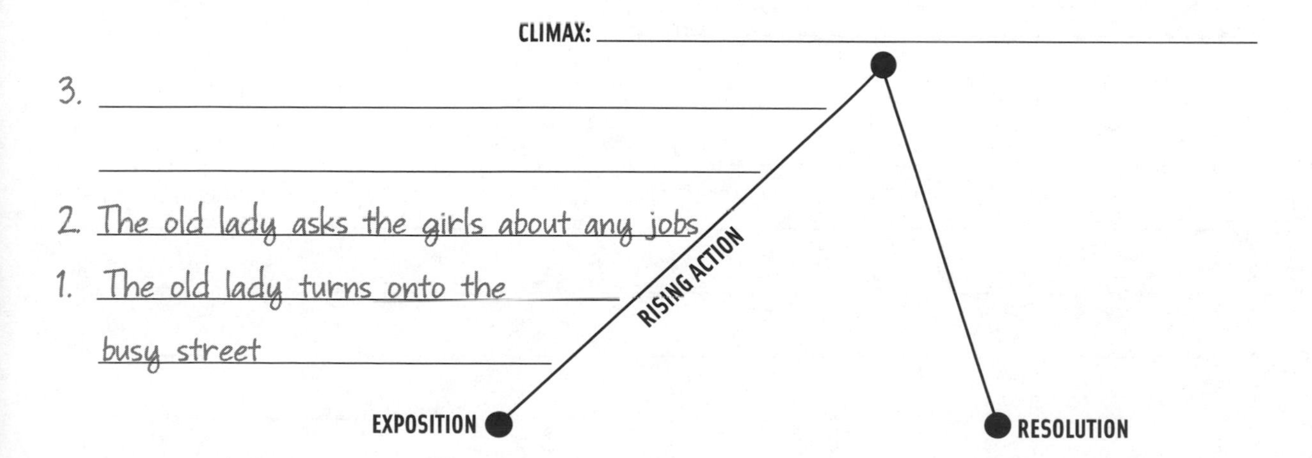

The sentences below describe how the first event helps create suspense. Write two or three sentences telling how the second event builds suspense.

The old lady hesitates after turning onto the loud and busy street. The event suggests the lady is out of her element. It builds suspense as readers begin to wonder why she is there.

Write a topic sentence stating the main idea of your response to the prompt.

Topic sentence:

Write ->

Explain how the suspense builds as events lead up to the climax of "A Detail." Support your answer by identifying the climax and three events in the rising action.

Scoring Standards

Your answer will be scored based on the standards below. Review your writing. If it doesn't meet the standard, you won't receive the highest score. Revise to improve your response. If necessary, rewrite it on another piece of paper.

Content > Does the response answer the question accurately and completely?

Does it

_____ tell how the suspense builds?
_____ identify the climax?
_____ identify three events in the rising action?
_____ include a clear topic sentence?
_____ provide enough details to support the topic sentence?
_____ stay on the topic without including details that do not support the main idea?

Organization > Is the response clearly and logically organized?

Does it

_____ present ideas in an order that makes the answer easy to understand?
_____ include transitions to make the sequence of events clear?

Voice and Style > Does the response show skillful use of language?

Does it

_____ display vivid and precise word choices?
_____ use a variety of sentence structures, such as simple, compound, and complex sentences?
_____ use a tone appropriate to the topic and test situation?

Now, check your writing against the editing checklist below.

Mechanics

_____ capitalization
_____ punctuation
_____ spelling
_____ sentence fragments
_____ subject-verb agreement
_____ consistency of verb tenses
_____ paragraphing
_____ run-on sentences

Lesson 9: Tone

Develop Your Skills –>

Tone is the author's attitude or feeling toward the subject or the audience. It may be formal, sad, angry, playful, friendly, bitter, or humorous, for example. Writers create tone through their choice of words and phrases as well as in the details they choose to give. For example, they may use slang or formal language. They may use exaggeration or jokes. They may use facts, examples, or descriptions that create a certain mood. Tone may remain the same throughout a piece of writing, or it may change in different passages.

Use a cluster diagram to gather words or details from a passage that suggest the writer's tone. Then look at the details and decide what general or overall tone they reflect.

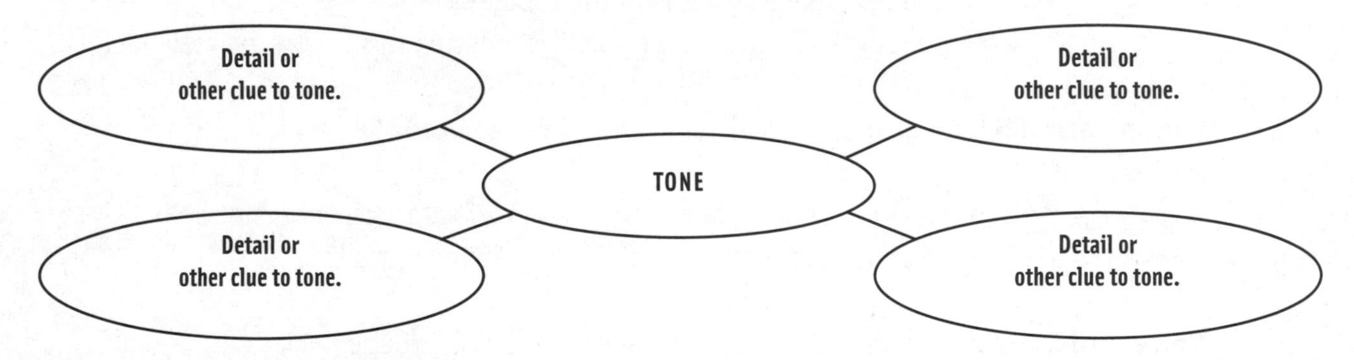

Read –>

"We Are Coming, Father Abraham"

by James Sloan Gibbons

This Civil War song first appeared as a poem in 1862. It was later put to music and became a popular Civil War song. It was often used for recruiting soldiers into the Union Army. "Father Abraham" refers to President Abraham Lincoln.

We are coming, Father Abra'am, six hundred thousand more,
From Mississippi's winding stream and from New England's shore;
We leave our plows and workshops our wives and children dear,
With hearts too full for utterance with but a silent tear;
Oh we dare not look behind us, but steadfastly before—
We are coming, Father Abra'am With six hundred thousand more!

Chorus:

We are coming, we are coming, Our Union to restore;
We are coming, Father Abra'am With Six hundred thousand more.

If you look across the hill tops that meet the northern sky,
Long moving lines of rising dust your vision may descry;
And now the wind an instant, tears the cloudy veil aside,
And floats aloft our spangled flag in glory and in pride;
And bayonets in the sunlight gleam, and bands brave music pour—
We are coming, Father Abra'am With six hundred thousand more!

If you look all up our valleys, Where the growing harvests shine,
You may see our sturdy farmer boys fast forming into line;
And children from their mother's knees are pulling at the weeds,
And learning how to reap and sow against their country's needs;
And a farewell group stand weeping at every cottage door—
We are coming, Father Abra'am With six hundred thousand more!

You have call'd us, and we're coming, by Richmond's bloody tide,
To lay us down for freedom's sake, our brothers' bones beside;
Or from foul treason's savage grasp to wrench the murderous blade,
And in the face of foreign foes its fragments to parade;
Six hundred thousand loyal men and true have gone before—
We are coming, Father Abra'am With six hundred thousand more!

What is the overall tone of the song? Explain your answer and give four words, phrases, or details from the song that help create this tone.

Plan —>

This cluster diagram analyzes the tone of the song. It provides two details that give clues to the author's attitude. The diagram already shows the tone they help create. Add two more details from the song that also develop this tone.

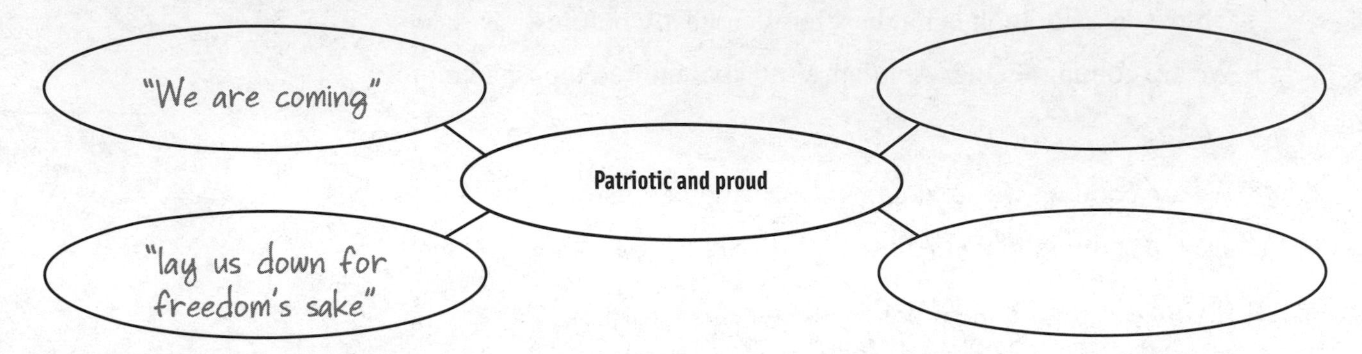

These model sentences explain how the words and details help create the tone.

The words "We are coming" show pride in what people are doing for the Union. The line "lay us down for freedom's sake" shows that people are willing to die for their country.

Look back at the question that follows the reading passage. Write a sentence that states the main idea of your answer. Use words from the prompt. This will be the topic sentence of your essay.

Topic sentence:

Write ->

Write your answer to the test question below. **What is the overall tone of the song? Explain your answer and give four words, phrases, or details from the song that help create this tone.** The answer has been started for you. It begins with the topic sentence and a transition sentence.

The overall tone of the song is patriotic and proud. Several phrases help create the tone.

____

____

____

____

____

____

Review and Edit ->

Scoring Standards

Review and revise your writing based on the standards below. Then, check your answer for errors in spelling, grammar, and usage.

Content > Does the response answer the question accurately and completely?
Does it

_____ state the overall tone of the song?
_____ identify four words, phrases, or details that create the tone?
_____ explain how the details help create the tone?
_____ include a clear topic sentence?
_____ stay on the topic without including details that do not support the main idea?

Organization > Is the response clearly and logically organized?
Does it

_____ organize ideas so the answer is easy to understand?

Voice and Style > Does the response show skillful use of language?
Does it

_____ display vivid and precise word choices?
_____ use a tone appropriate to the topic and test situation?

Apply Your Skills –>

Read –>

"Ain't I A Woman?"

by Sojourner Truth

Sojourner Truth (1797–1883) was born into slavery, but later earned her freedom. She became one of the most outspoken leaders in the movements to end slavery and to win greater rights for women. Throughout the 19th century, women had fewer rights than men. They could not vote in national elections or in state and local elections in most states. Their rights to own property were restricted. And they lacked many of the social and cultural rights women today take for granted. Truth delivered this speech at a historic Women's Convention in December 1851 in Akron, Ohio. She raises important questions in her fight for women's rights.

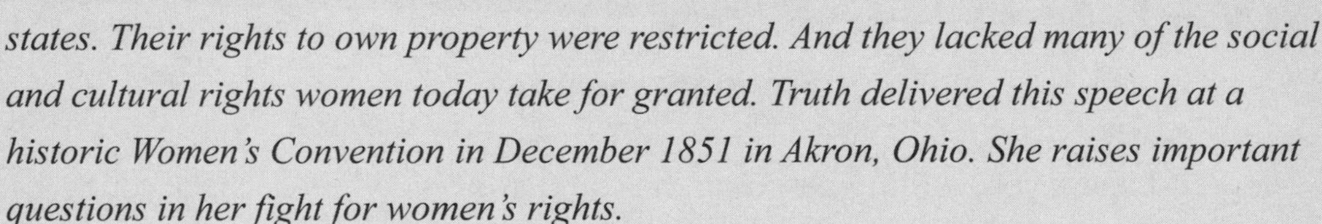

Well, children, where there is so much racket there must be something out of kilter. I think that 'twixt the negroes of the South and the women at the North, all talking about rights, the white men will be in a fix pretty soon. But what's all this here talking about?

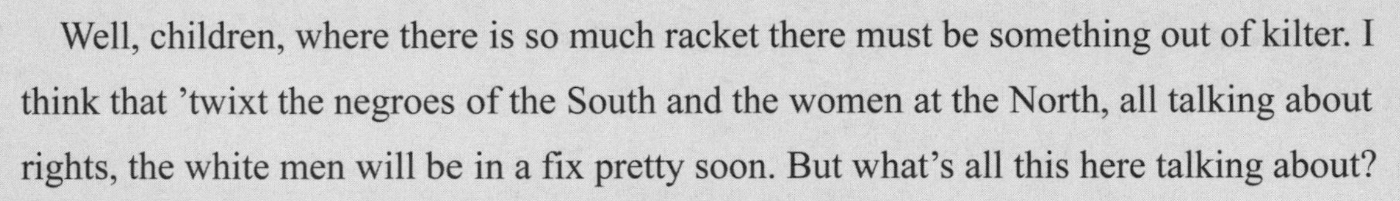

That man over there says that women need to be helped into carriages, and lifted over ditches, and to have the best place everywhere. Nobody ever helps me into carriages, or over mud-puddles, or gives me any best place! And ain't I a woman? Look at me! Look at my arm! I have ploughed and planted, and gathered into barns, and no man could head me! And ain't I a woman? I could work as much and eat as much as a man—when I could get it—and bear the lash as well! And ain't I a woman? I have borne thirteen children, and seen most all sold off to slavery, and when I cried out with my mother's grief, none but Jesus heard me! And ain't I a woman?

Then they talk about this thing in the head; what's this they call it? [a member of the

audience calls out, "intellect"] That's it, honey. What's that got to do with women's rights or negroes' rights? If my cup won't hold but a pint, and yours holds a quart, wouldn't you be mean not to let me have my little half measure full?

Then that little man in black there, he says women can't have as much rights as men, 'cause Christ wasn't a woman! Where did your Christ come from? Where did your Christ come from? From God and a woman! Man had nothing to do with Him.

If the first woman God ever made was strong enough to turn the world upside down all alone, these women together ought to be able to turn it back, and get it right side up again! And now they is asking to do it, the men better let them.

Obliged to you for hearing me, and now old Sojourner ain't got nothing more to say.

Identify Sojourner Truth's tone in this speech. Is it formal or informal? Explain how her choice of words and details helps develop the tone. Analyze two word choices, an example, and a question from her speech.

Plan →

This graphic organizer analyzes the tone of Sojourner Truth's speech. Complete the organizer.

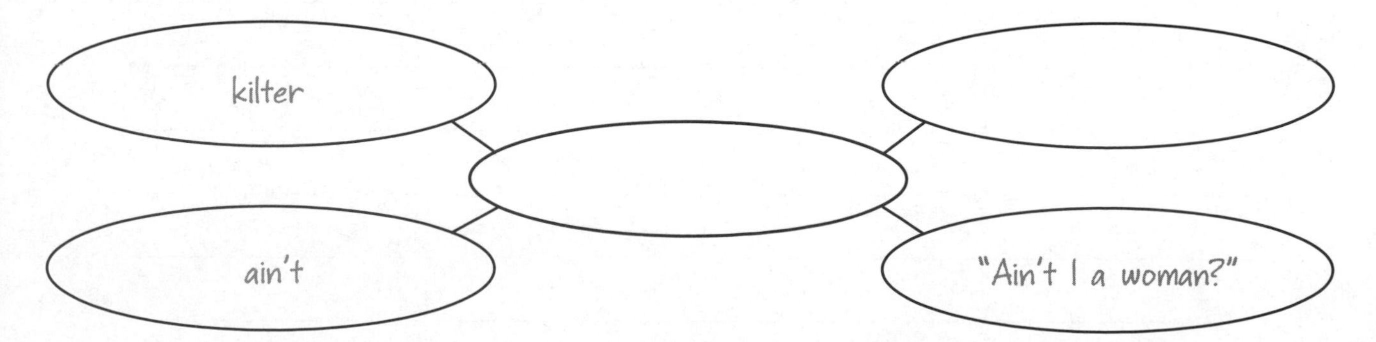

The model sentences explain how the word choices help create an informal tone.

Sojourner Truth's tone is informal because she uses such words as "kilter" and "ain't." When something is "out of kilter" it is not right. "Ain't" is slang. People don't use these words in formal speech.

Now, write one or two sentences telling how Truth's question helps develop her tone.

Write a topic sentence stating the main idea of your response to the question.

Topic sentence:

Write →

Identify Sojourner Truth's tone in this speech. Is it formal or informal? Explain how her choice of words and details helps develop the tone. Analyze two word choices, an example, and a question from her speech.

Scoring Standards

Your answer will be scored based on the standards below. Review your writing. If it doesn't meet the standard, you won't receive the highest score. Revise to improve your response. If necessary, rewrite it on another piece of paper.

Content > Does the response answer the question accurately and completely?

Does it

______ state the overall tone of the speech?
______ explain how word choices and details help create the tone?
______ cite two word choices, an example, and a question that develop the tone?
______ include a clear topic sentence?
______ provide enough details to support the topic sentence?
______ stay on the topic without including details that do not support the main idea?

Organization > Is the response clearly and logically organized?

Does it

______ present ideas in an order that makes the answer easy to understand?
______ include transitions to make the relationships among ideas clear?

Voice and Style > Does the response show skillful use of language?

Does it

______ display vivid and precise word choices?
______ use a variety of sentence structures, such as simple, compound, and complex sentences?
______ use a tone appropriate to the topic and test situation?

Now, check your writing against the editing checklist below.

Mechanics

______ capitalization
______ punctuation
______ spelling
______ sentence fragments
______ subject-verb agreement
______ consistency of verb tenses
______ paragraphing
______ run-on sentences

THE BIRTH OF FRANKENSTEIN'S MONSTER

The creature known as Frankenstein's monster was created by a young woman named Mary Shelley. She brought the monster into the world in 1816. It has haunted our imagination and dreams ever since.

Mary Shelley was 19 when she invented the monster. She was the wife of poet Percy Shelley. Percy Shelley was just 24, but he was already a leading poet of the period. The Shelleys went to Switzerland on a summer vacation, where they stayed on the shores of Lake Geneva. Lord Byron, another great poet, was staying nearby. Dr. John Polidori, Byron's friend and personal doctor, was staying with Byron. The four spent time together. They went boating on the lake and took long walks on the shore. But it was a wet summer, so the group often stayed indoors. Then, Mary Shelly remembers, "Some volumes of ghost stories . . . fell into our hands." They spent a long evening at Byron's where they talked and read ghost stories to each other. Byron was the unofficial leader of the group. He challenged each of his friends to write a ghost story. They quickly agreed.

At 28, Byron was the oldest of the four and was the most famous and widely published. He quickly hit upon an idea for his own story and began writing. It was about two men traveling in a distant country. One mysteriously dies and withers before the eyes of his friend. Although easily begun, the project quickly died as Byron lost interest. He never finished it.

Percy Shelley also came up with an idea without trouble. It was drawn from his early life. Like his friend Byron, he soon lost interest in the story and gave it up. Mary Shelley explained that her husband was used to writing poetry rich in imagery. Putting words into prose and creating a plot may have bored him.

Remember the steps:

Read
Plan
Write
Review & Edit

A young man of just 20, Dr. Polidori must have felt somewhat overwhelmed. Although bright and well educated, he was a doctor, not a writer. And here he was, competing with two of the great poets of the century. So he did not immediately begin writing. He probably had trouble finding a subject. But when Byron gave up on his story, Polidori picked it up. With Byron's approval, he used it as the basis of his own story. He called it "The Vampyre."

Mary Shelley, like Dr. Polidori, was not a successful writer. But she had been around writers all her life. She grew up in a literary family. Her father was a writer and political reformer. Her mother was also a writer and was one of the first feminists. Mary never knew her mother, who died in childbirth. Still, the memory and achievements of her mother must have left an impression on Mary. In addition, she grew up in a home where she was encouraged to learn. That was unusual for girls at this time. Plus, she was used to being around writers and intellectuals. But she had trouble thinking of an idea for her ghost story. She worried that she wouldn't think of anything.

Then several days later, she had her inspiration. Byron and Percy Shelley were talking about a scientific experiment that was in the news. A doctor was using electricity to make the dissected legs of animals move. Perhaps, they thought, this might be a way to create life. Or maybe an animal could be built by combining different parts. The discussion fired Mary Shelley's imagination.

"When I placed my head on my pillow," Shelley recalled, "I did not sleep, nor could I be said to think. My imagination . . . guided me." She saw a monster that some doctor had made from the parts of dead people. Then she saw it stretched out on a table. She imagined some huge machine and how it gave life to the monster. In the morning, Shelley could not forget the things she imagined. She sat down and wrote the story of Frankenstein's monster.

Mary Shelley's work was the only truly successful piece written by the group. Nothing came of her husband's effort. Byron later published the fragment he had begun, but it is not remarkable. Polidori's "The Vampyre" was the first modern story of vampires in English literature. It inspired many of the later stories of vampires. But Mary Shelley's *Frankenstein* has become a classic. It has been made into many films and comic books. It has inspired new books and studies by scholars. She was probably the least likely of the four friends to write a great story. Yet she created the most important and the most enduring.

1. How are Mary Shelley's and Polidori's stories alike and different?

2. Based on information in the passage, which two of the four friends seem to have the most in common? Explain your choice.

3. Compare and contrast the efforts of the four friends to write ghost stories.

____

____

____

____

____

____

____

____

____

____

____

____

____

____

Checklist

Content, Organization, and Style

_____ Accurate, complete response
_____ Similarities
_____ Differences
_____ Supporting details
_____ Logical organization
_____ Vivid, precise word choices
_____ Appropriate tone

Spelling, Grammar, and Usage

_____ Capitalization
_____ Punctuation
_____ Spelling
_____ Fragments and run-on sentences
_____ Subject and verb agreement
_____ Consistent verb tenses
_____ Correct paragraphs

"How the Camel Got His Hump"

by Rudyard Kipling

Now this is the next tale, and it tells how the Camel got his big hump.

In the beginning of years, when the world was so new-and-all, and the Animals were just beginning to work for Man, there was a Camel, and he lived in the middle of a Howling Desert because he did not want to work; and besides, he was a Howler himself. So he ate sticks and thorns and tamarisks and milkweed and prickles, most 'scruciating idle; and when anybody spoke to him he said "Humph!" Just "Humph!" and no more.

Presently the Horse came to him on Monday morning, with a saddle on his back and a bit in his mouth, and said, "Camel, O Camel, come out and trot like the rest of us."

"Humph!" said the Camel; and the Horse went away and told the Man.

Presently the Dog came to him, with a stick in his mouth, and said, "Camel, O Camel, come and fetch and carry like the rest of us."

"Humph!" said the Camel; and the Dog went away and told the Man.

Presently the Ox came to him, with the yoke on his neck, and said, "Camel, O Camel, come and plough like the rest of us."

"Humph!" said the Camel; and the Ox went away and told the Man.

At the end of the day the Man called the Horse and the Dog and the Ox together, and said, "Three, O Three, I'm very sorry for you (with the world so new-and-all); but that Humph-thing in the Desert can't work, or he would have been here by now, so I am going to leave him alone, and you must work double-time to make up for it."

That made the Three very angry (with the world so new-and-all), and they held a palaver, and an indaba, and a punchayet, and a pow-wow on the edge of the Desert; and the Camel came chewing milkweed most 'scruciating idle, and laughed at them. Then he said "Humph!" and went away again.

Presently there came along the Djinn in charge of All Deserts, rolling in a cloud of dust (Djinns always travel that way because it is Magic), and he stopped to palaver and pow-wow with the Three.

"Djinn of All Deserts," said the Horse, "is it right for any one to be idle, with the world so new-and-all?"

"Certainly not," said the Djinn.

"Well," said the Horse, "there's a thing in the middle of your Howling Desert (and he's a Howler himself) with a long neck and long legs, and he hasn't done a stroke of work since Monday morning. He won't trot."

"Whew!" said the Djinn, whistling, "that's my Camel, for all the gold in Arabia! What does he say about it?"

"He says 'Humph!'" said the Dog; "and he won't fetch and carry."

"Does he say anything else?"

"Only 'Humph!'; and he won't plough," said the Ox.

"Very good," said the Djinn. "I'll humph him if you will kindly wait a minute."

The Djinn rolled himself up in his dust-cloak, and took a bearing across the desert, and found the Camel most 'scruciatingly idle, looking at his own reflection in a pool of water.

"My long and bubbling friend," said the Djinn, "what's this I hear of your doing no work, with the world so new-and-all?"

"Humph!" said the Camel.

The Djinn sat down, with his chin in his hand,

and began to think a Great Magic, while the Camel looked at his own reflection in the pool of water.

"You've given the Three extra work ever since Monday morning, all on account of your 'scruciating idleness," said the Djinn; and he went on thinking Magics, with his chin in his hand.

"Humph!" said the Camel.

"I shouldn't say that again if I were you," said the Djinn; "you might say it once too often. Bubbles, I want you to work."

And the Camel said "Humph!" again; but no sooner had he said it than he saw his back, that he was so proud of, puffing up and puffing up into a great big lolloping humph.

"Do you see that?" said the Djinn. "That's your very own humph that you've brought upon your very own self by not working. To-day is Thursday, and you've done no work since Monday, when the work began. Now you are going to work."

"How can I," said the Camel, "with this humph on my back?"

"That's made a-purpose," said the Djinn, "all because you missed those three days. You will be able to work now for three days without eating, because you can live on your humph; and don't you ever say I never did anything for you. Come out of the Desert and go to the Three, and behave. Humph yourself!"

And the Camel humphed himself, humph and all, and went away to join the Three. And from that day to this the Camel always wears a humph (we call it "hump" now, not to hurt his feelings); but he has never yet caught up with the three days that he missed at the beginning of the world, and he has never yet learned how to behave.

1. What information does Rudyard Kipling provide in the story's exposition?

2. What takes place during the resolution of the story?

3. When does the climax of the story occur? Using details from the story, explain how you know.

____

____

____

____

____

____

____

____

____

____

____

____

____

____

Checklist

Content, Organization, and Style

_____ Accurate, complete response
_____ Main idea
_____ Most important details
_____ Ideas restated in your own words
_____ Topic sentence
_____ Logical organization
_____ Vivid, precise word choices
_____ Appropriate tone

Spelling, Grammar, and Usage

_____ Capitalization
_____ Punctuation
_____ Spelling
_____ Fragments and run-on sentences
_____ Subject and verb agreement
_____ Consistent verb tenses
_____ Correct paragraphs

COMICS IN THE CLASSROOM?

Comic books have come a long way in the last fifty years. In 1954, Frederic Wertham wrote a book called *Seduction of the Innocent.* He claimed comic books ruined the morals of young people. Plus, they destroyed children's sense of literature and art. Comic books had never had a great reputation. Wertham's criticism made it even worse. Parents clamped down on their children for reading such rubbish. Sales of comics crashed.

In the years since, comic book sales have slowly come back. Meanwhile, comics have become almost respectable. Some schools even use them in the classroom. Maryland, for example, is starting a program for students from kindergarten through high school. Comic books will not replace the normal reading materials. They will be used to add to what is offered.

Even colleges and universities are bringing in comic books. Palomar College in San Marcos, California, and the State University at Canton, New York, give courses on graphic novels, as comics are now being called.

Can't you just hear the sighs and moans coming from moms and dads when they hear this about their local schools? "Is this why we send our kids to school—to read comic books?" they ask. "Is this why we pay taxes to support public schools?"

I guess the answers to these questions are, yes. But let's not overreact. Comic books have come a long way in 50 years. They're respectable. In 1992, a Pulitzer Prize was awarded to Art Spiegelman for his *Maus.* This comic book told a story about surviving the holocaust. And in 2001, Michael Chabon received the Pulitzer for *The Amazing Adventures of Kavalier & Clay.* It's a story about the comic book industry before World War II. Pulitzers are serious awards. They're given to writers who have produced highly artistic works. So when people talk about comic books, they're no longer talking about literary trash. At least some of them rise above that level.

Is it possible then that comics, or graphic novels if you prefer, really are literature? Do they belong on the same bookshelf with Charles Dickens's *Oliver Twist* or Ernest Hemingway's *The Sun Also Rises?* Does this justify bringing them into the classroom? Maybe. At least that's one view. The fact is, however, that few comic books reach the literary levels of *Maus* and *Kavalier & Clay.*

Teachers have a better reason for using comic books in school. A survey by the National Assessment of Education Progress shows that fewer and fewer Americans between the ages of 13 and 17 read for fun. It's not that they can't read. They can, but they choose not to. Part of the problem is that other activities get in the way. People prefer to play sports and video games. They'd rather watch movies or just hang out with friends.

Newspape

books, and magazines can't compete with this. Can you just see a kid turning down a chance to watch a new video with a friend? "Sorry, I'd rather curl up with this great novel I'm reading. It's called *Moby Dick.*" That's just not going to happen.

On the other hand, someone might put off a game of basketball to read a comic book. Or more likely still, she'll just lean against the goal post and read it while she waits for the gang to gather. So comic books might be a way to reach students. They might help get kids interested in reading. Maybe *Starman* and *Justice League of America* aren't great literature. But any kind of reading is better than no reading at all. Right?

That seems to be the thinking of the New York City Comic Book Museum. They got together with the Metropolitan Transit Authority, Landmark High School, and the New York Explorer Program. Together, they gave away comic books to people riding the subway. They called their program "Reading on the Move: Ride the Subway—Read a Comic." And its purpose was plain and simple. Give people something they'll enjoy reading. Just getting into the habit of reading anything is a step in the right direction.

Comics are a useful tool in the classroom for one more reason. They're a great way to teach kids about fiction. Just like novels and short stories, comic books have characters, plots, conflicts, themes, and the other elements of fiction. They're just not as complex. It's easier to understand the elements of a story when a million other details aren't confusing the issue. Teachers can always take things to the next level. They can have students apply the same skills to something bigger and "better." Comic books, though, are a great way to start.

So here's a vote for the teachers who bring comic books into the classroom. You're doing the right thing. You're inspiring your students. You're helping them get started on reading. You're giving them a reason for reading. You're helping them learn to enjoy it. Hey, what more can anyone do?

1. According to this essay, what is Frederick Wertham's attitude toward comics? Explain how you know.

2. What is the writer's attitude toward comics? Give at least three examples from the essay to support your answer.

3. Identify the overall tone of the article and tell how the writer develops it through a choice of words and details. Cite at least five words or details from the article to support your answer.

____

____

____

____

____

____

____

____

____

____

____

____

____

____

Checklist

Content, Organization, and Style

_____ Accurate, complete response
_____ Sequence of events clear
_____ Topic sentence
_____ Supporting details
_____ Logical organization
_____ Transitional words
_____ Vivid, precise word choices
_____ Appropriate tone

Spelling, Grammar, and Usage

_____ Capitalization
_____ Punctuation
_____ Spelling
_____ Fragments and run-on sentences
_____ Subject and verb agreement
_____ Consistent verb tenses
_____ Correct paragraphs

There's a Moose in My Driveway!

Andrew Shelffo lives in downtown Northampton, Massachusetts. One day, he was quietly drinking coffee on his back porch. Then, according to a report in the *Christian Science Monitor,* a dark shape suddenly loomed up in front of him. It was six-feet tall at the shoulders and standing in the middle of his driveway. "At first," he told a reporter, "I just thought 'Holy cow, there's a moose in my driveway!'" Then he wondered if he should grab a camera so he could prove to neighbors that he actually saw one.

Stories like Shelffo's shouldn't be that hard to believe anymore. Wildlife has been showing up in ever greater numbers in cities throughout the United States. Wildlife services in Boston have had to deal with skunks, bats, deer, raccoons, seals, moose, and swans. Bears have been seen in Connecticut neighborhoods. Black bears can live for up to 30 years. Police shot a mountain lion that had retreated into a tree in California's crowded Silicon Valley. And coyotes can show up on doorsteps almost anywhere.

Back where they belong

So why are we seeing so many wild animals in our cities? There are several answers. First, we should remember that wild animals have always lived in America. Most of the animals in our cities are not new. They're simply coming back to places where they used to live.

The first few hundred years of this country's history were hard on animals. Vast forests were cut down for farms, ranches, and cities. Native grasslands were plowed under. Until the early 1900s, there were few laws about hunting. People shot as many deer and bison as they wanted. Vast numbers were killed. All these factors took their toll. For many years deer and turkey were rare, seen only by luck in the most remote places.

But then federal and state governments started controlling hunting. They also worked to bring back animals. Many species have rebounded. In the meantime, conservation areas were established. Trees were planted. Animals were brought back to these places and protected. In more recent decades, cities have begun adding parklands. Greenways—long, narrow parks—have been built that link parks and connect to rural areas. Animals now find good habitat along the edges and even in the heart of most cities.

At the same time, our cities are growing. People are building houses in places that were farmland just a few years before. The wild animals are still there, trying to live as they have always lived.

Good neighbors, bad neighbors

Most people enjoy seeing a moose in their driveway or a deer in their backyard. Usually there's no harm. Sometimes, though, wild animals and people don't mix. Deer graze on garden plants. Raccoons overturn trash cans and spread garbage up and down the block. Canada geese are loud, aggressive, and messy.

In some cases, wild animals pose more serious problems. Coyotes have adapted very well to living around humans. Usually, we don't know they're around. But sometimes, they may carry off pets that are left alone in backyards. And while attacks on people are extremely rare, they've happened. There have been 160 serious coyote encounters in California in the last 30 years.

Peaceful coexistence

So what do we do about the wild animals in our midst? First, enjoy them. There are few things as inspiring as seeing a full-grown moose in your driveway. Second, remember that they're wild animals. Keep your distance and respect their need for space. Even small animals, like raccoons, can deliver a nasty bite or scratch. If animals are acting aggressively, notify an animal control officer.

If animals are simply a nuisance, you may also call in the experts for help. But sometimes, the problem is too big. An exploding population of deer or Canada geese can be a problem with no easy answers. Hunting may be an option. But many people don't want to see the animals killed. Besides, hunting in urban areas presents huge problems on its own. Often, government agencies try to trap the animals and move them to new places. This may work for a while, but it's only a short-term answer.

Most often, there is no entirely satisfactory solution. The animals are just living where and how they can. When people are around, the animals try to adapt. At the same time, people are doing what people do, spreading out and building their homes in all kinds of places. Contact between animals and people can't be avoided. Both are here to stay. In most cases, the best thing we can do is simply learn to get along.

1. In paragraph 2, which detail does not support the main idea? Give reasons for your choice.

____

____

____

____

____

____

____

____

2. What is the main idea of the section, "Back where they belong"? Give three details from the section to support your answer.

____

____

____

____

3. **Explain how the main idea of each section supports the main idea of the whole article.**

Is There Really a Neverland?

The play *Peter Pan; or The Boy Who Would Not Grow Up,* was first performed in 1904. It is possibly the most popular play ever written for children.

The play is about a boy, Peter Pan, who never grows up. He can fly and talk to fairies. He fights pirates and lives with Indians. We first meet him when he flies into the home of the Darlings. He is searching for his shadow, which somehow got lost.

Peter finds it in the nursery occupied by the Darling children. As he unsuccessfully tries to reattach the shadow, the children awaken. Wendy, the eldest, sews it back on for him.

And this launches the story. Peter and Wendy and her little brothers become friends. Peter teaches them to fly, and together they fly back to his home in Neverland. It's easy to find, he says. You simply fly toward the stars—"the second to the right, and straight on till morning."

Neverland is an island far away. Peter lives there with the Lost Boys. Their neighbors include pirates, Indians, fairies, mermaids, and elves. Peter is the leader of the Lost Boys, and Wendy becomes their temporary mother. The boys are in constant battle with the pirates.

The pirates are led by Captain Hook. He is missing one hand, which Peter cut off long ago in a sword fight. The hand fell into the water where a crocodile ate it along with Hook's watch. The crocodile liked Hook's hand so well that he always follows Hook around, hoping for more. Hook knows when the crocodile is near because he can hear his watch still ticking. Although Hook is the chief villain, he is not completely evil. He is sorry that the children do not like him, and he treats Wendy with respect.

Like any boy, Peter has a taste for adventure and a short memory. After defeating Captain Hook, he quickly forgets about Hook and the danger he was in. Instead he sets off on new adventures with new dangers. And if he should die, that's all right. "Death," he says, "would be a great adventure."

Wendy, meantime, goes home to her family. But the story never ends because Peter refuses to grow up. Each year, while Wendy remains a child, Peter comes to get her, and he takes her home with him to Neverland. When she grows up, she can no longer fly. She has a child, though, a girl named Jane. When Jane is old enough, she goes to Neverland with Peter. And when Jane grows up, her daughter Margaret learns to fly away with Peter. And "thus it will go on . . . so long as children are gay and innocent and heartless."

J.M. Barrie created the story of Peter Pan sometime after 1898 when he became close to the family of Sylvia and Arthur Llewelyn Davies. He often played with the five Davies children and told them stories. When the parents died in 1908 and 1910, Barrie became even closer to the children, helping to raise them almost as if they were his own. The story of Peter Pan evolved from stories he told the Davies children when they were very small.

The roots of the story may go back to Barrie's childhood. He was born in 1860, the ninth child in a family of ten. Barrie's brother, his mother's favorite, died when Barrie was seven. She mourned and fell into a deep depression. Barrie tried to become the child she had lost. In some ways, it may have stunted his growth into adulthood as he tried to remain a child to ease his mother's suffering. This, of course, is just a guess. But Barrie's fascination with children and childhood remained with him throughout his life.

The story Barrie created is about a boy who wants to hold onto childhood. He lives in Neverland, a fantasy world occupied by children and their dreams of adventure. It is a place that only children can go because it exists only in the imagination. Adults lose that ability to imagine such fantastic places and to dream of impossible things. At least most of them lose that ability. There are a few who are forever children in some ways. People like J.M. Barrie never entirely grow up. They can always imagine their way back to Neverland. For children and adults like Barrie, this land of the imagination remains forever real.

4. Using four details from the passage, tell how Neverland is the same as and different from the real world.

5. Compare and contrast Peter Pan to a real boy. Tell whether you think they are more alike or more different. Include six details from the passage to support your answer.

Otzi the Ice Man

In September 1991, two people were hiking in the Alps, high in the mountains along the border of Austria and Italy. They hiked into a pass through the mountains. There, they stumbled upon a shocking discovery—the head and shoulders of a man were sticking up above the melting ice of a glacier.

The hikers thought they had found the body of a lost hiker. They went for help and brought back rescue workers. The rescue team cut the body out of the ice, took it to Innsbruck, Austria, and examined it.

Later, people realized that this was no ordinary hiker. It was the body of a man who had died 5,300 years before. They named the body Otzi (which rhymes with *tootsie*) after the area where it was found. It was an amazing discovery. Never before had a complete body been found from so long ago. In the past, scientists had only found skeletons and scattered bones. With Otzi, scientists also found clothing, a copper ax, a bow and arrows, a cap, and other belongings. These items provided a snapshot of life 5,300 years ago.

Scientists ran tests and learned that the body was that of a man who was probably in his 40s when he died. That made him quite old for a person of his time. Scientists also found two injuries. A stone arrowhead was lodged in Otzi's back, and he had a deep cut in his right hand. Both injuries probably occurred within hours before his death.

The mystery

Of course, many questions arise. What was Otzi doing so high in the mountains? How did he die? No evidence exists that will completely answer these questions, but scientists do have several ideas.

One of the most convincing theories is that Otzi was murdered by rivals. Some scientists think he may have been a leader. He might have been a shaman, or spiritual leader and healer. His body has more than 50 tattoos. Tattoos are sometimes associated with shamans in some cultures.

Otzi also carried a pouch containing medicines and a copper ax. Such an ax was valuable and likely belonged to an important leader. It could be that other members of his group were trying to take over. If he didn't want to give up his position, his rivals may have followed him into the mountains and attacked him. They may first have attacked with a knife. He fought back, getting a deep cut on his hand. Then, as he ran away, one of them shot him in the back with an arrow. Otzi pulled the shaft of the arrow out, but the arrowhead remained in his shoulder. Scientists can tell that the wound in his hand occurred from three to eight days before his death. So although he got away, his wounds were serious. Besides, the mountains were freezing cold. He may have died from the combination of severe weather, hunger, and his wounds.

Another theory suggests that Otzi was a herdsman who followed his animals to this high elevation in the summer. So he knew the area well. From the food found in his stomach, scientists believe his last meal was eaten in a valley at a lower elevation. Otzi ate the food about eight hours before he died. So some scientists think his village may have been attacked by a warring group. Blood from four different people was found on his clothing and on one arrow. So he was not the only one bleeding. He was probably injured in the conflict. As a result, he fled, according to this theory, and sought refuge in the high mountains. There, he died from his wounds.

Still another theory suggests that Otzi was a hunter. His weapons may have been those of a highly skilled hunter who hunted in these high mountains. Mountains, in those days, were often the dividing line between different groups. So maybe he came into conflict with a competing group. Again the blood on his clothing suggests he was in a fight. Some scientists think he may have been carrying a comrade. That would explain why he had someone else's blood on the back of his coat. The fact that his copper ax was with him suggests that he may have escaped his attackers only to die alone.

Of course, we'll never know for sure what happened to Otzi. The evidence can be interpreted many ways. Each of the theories seems logical. But which is correct? Did something else happen? It's impossible to say, but it probably doesn't really matter anyway. What Otzi has given us is a snapshot of life 5,300 years ago. The questions never stop, but just by asking them, we come closer to understanding a little about life thousands of years ago.

6. In the final lines the writer says that what happened to Otzi isn't really important. What is important is the understanding we gained about life long ago. Explain how the discovery of the body led to this knowledge.

____

____

____

____

____

____

____

____

7. Why do some scientists think Otzi was an important leader? Give at least two reasons.

____

____

____

____

____

____

____

____

8. **Scientists have several theories about how and why Otzi died. Which theory is the most convincing? Give at least five details from the article to explain your answer.**

"The Story of an Hour"

By Kate Chopin

Knowing that Mrs. Mallard was afflicted with a heart trouble, great care was taken to break to her as gently as possible the news of her husband's death.

It was her sister Josephine who told her, in broken sentences; veiled hints that revealed in half concealing. Her husband's friend Richards was there, too, near her. It was he who had been in the newspaper office when intelligence of the railroad disaster was received, with Brently Mallard's name leading the list of "killed." He had only taken the time to assure himself of its truth by a second telegram, and had hastened to forestall any less careful, less tender friend in bearing the sad message.

She did not hear the story as many women have heard the same, with a paralyzed inability to accept its significance. She wept at once, with sudden, wild abandonment, in her sister's arms. When the storm of grief had spent itself she went away to her room alone. She would have no one follow her.

There stood, facing the open window, a comfortable, roomy armchair. Into this she sank, pressed down by a physical exhaustion that haunted her body and seemed to reach into her soul. . . .

She sat with her head thrown back upon the cushion of the chair, quite motionless, except when a sob came up into her throat and shook her, as a child who has cried itself to sleep continues to sob in its dreams. . . .

There was something coming to her and she was waiting for it, fearfully. What was it? She did not know; it was too subtle and elusive to name. But she felt it, creeping out of the sky, reaching toward her through the sounds, the scents, the color that filled the air.

Now her bosom rose and fell tumultuously. She was beginning to recognize this thing that was approaching to possess her, and she was striving to beat it back with her will—as powerless as her two white slender hands would have been.

When she abandoned herself a little whispered word escaped her slightly parted lips. She said it over and over under her breath: "free, free, free!" The vacant stare and the look of terror that had followed it went from her eyes. They stayed keen and bright. Her pulses beat fast, and the coursing blood warmed and relaxed every inch of her body.

She did not stop to ask if it were or were not a monstrous joy that held her. A clear and exalted perception enabled her to dismiss the suggestion as trivial.

She knew that she would weep again when she saw the kind, tender hands folded in death; the face that had never looked save with love upon her, fixed and gray and dead. But she saw beyond that bitter moment a long procession of years to come that would belong to her absolutely. And she opened and spread her arms out to them in welcome.

There would be no one to live for during those coming years; she would live for herself. There would be no powerful will bending hers in that blind persistence with which men and women believe they have a right to impose a private will upon a fellow-creature. A kind intention or a cruel intention made the act seem no less a crime as she looked upon it in that brief moment of illumination.

And yet she had loved him—sometimes. Often she had not. What did it matter! What could love, the unsolved mystery, count for in face of this possession of self-assertion which she suddenly recognized as the strongest impulse of her being!

"Free! Body and soul free!" she kept whispering.

Josephine was kneeling before the closed door with her lips to the keyhole, imploring for admission. "Louise, open the door! I beg, open the door—you will make yourself ill. What are you doing, Louise? For heaven's sake open the door."

"Go away. I am not making myself ill." No; she was drinking in a very elixir of life through that open window.

Her fancy was running riot along those days ahead of her. Spring days, and summer days, and all sorts of days that would be her own. She breathed a quick prayer that life might be long. It was only yesterday she had thought with a shudder that life might be long.

She arose at length and opened the door. . . . There was a feverish triumph in her eyes, and she carried herself unwittingly like a goddess of Victory. She clasped her sister's waist, and together they descended the stairs. Richards stood waiting for them at the bottom.

Some one was opening the front door with a latchkey. It was Brently Mallard who entered, a little travel-stained, composedly carrying his grip-sack and umbrella. He had been far from the scene of accident, and did not even know there had been one. He stood amazed at Josephine's piercing cry; at Richards' quick motion to screen him from the view of his wife.

But Richards was too late.

When the doctors came they said she had died of heart disease—of joy that kills.

9. When does the rising action begin? Give two details from the story to support your answer.

10. In many stories, the resolution covers several paragraphs, and sometimes more. Here the resolution is very short. Explain where the resolution occurs and tell what events make it up.

11. Explain where the climax occurs and how you know. Use four events in the rising action to support your response.

SALMON OR DAMS?

A hundred years ago, salmon thrived in the rivers of the northwestern United States. There seemed no limit to the number of salmon that could be caught. What seemed in short supply were water for irrigation and electric power for the cities.

This region lies along the Pacific Ocean. The westernmost part of this area gets lots of rain. But inland, little rain falls. It is nearly a desert, although the soil is rich. Farmers wanted to raise crops like corn and potatoes. These need much more rain than this land ever gets. To make it possible to grow these crops, farmers wanted to irrigate the land. That requires lots of water.

Meanwhile, the cities were growing. Homes and businesses needed electricity. Power-hungry industries needed huge amounts of electricity.

People saw a solution to these problems. It was the Columbia River and its major tributary, the Snake River. Beginning in 1938, the United States Army Corps of Engineers began building dams. They built 18 major and many smaller dams on the Columbia and Snake rivers. The dams did fulfill their mission. The lakes formed by the dams provided water for irrigation. Farmers of the arid lands could raise apples, potatoes, alfalfa, wheat, corn, beans, sugar beets, and other water-demanding crops.

The dams also produced great amounts of electric power. The dams created deep lakes. As the water was released, the flowing water turned turbines. These produced electricity. Today, these dams supply two-thirds of the electricity used by people in the Northwest. All this proves that the dams were a great idea, right?

Well, not quite. There is a good reason why the dams were a bad idea from the start. The reason has to do with salmon and the people whose lives depend on salmon. These fish breed and lay eggs in the upper reaches of the Columbia River system. After the eggs hatch, the young salmon travel down the river to the ocean. They live there from two to five years. Then they return to the same streams where they were born. They breed and lay eggs in these streams.

Fishing for salmon once provided jobs for people throughout the Northwest. It provided food for people across the United States. And for thousands of years, the salmon provided food for Native Americans. Fishing was central to their way of life. The dams, however, blocked the migration of salmon. The fish couldn't get up or down the river. In the 1930s, about 25 million pounds of fish were caught in the Columbia River system. Today, only one or two million pounds of fish are caught each year. Plus, about 10,000 jobs in the fishing industry have been lost. This happened because there are fewer fish. Much of the Native Americans' traditional fishing culture has been lost.

Most people accept that there's a problem. The government has spent hundreds of millions of dollars trying to save the fish. Workers have collected the young salmon, put them on barges, and taken them below the dams, where they released them. They have built ways for the salmon to pass around the dams. And they have tried other ideas. In fact, between 2000 and 2005, the government tried more than 200 ways to help the salmon. Nothing has worked. In fact, efforts to save the salmon have failed miserably. Twelve species of salmon are listed as threatened or endangered. That means they are at a high risk of disappearing forever.

Scientists say the best way of saving the salmon is to remove all the dams. And there has been serious talk about doing that. The dams have powerful friends, though. Farmers who want the water fight to keep the dams. Big businesses that use lots of energy want to protect them. Even if this ideal solution is taken, it is almost certainly a long way off.

However, just four dams on the lower Snake bear most of the blame for destroying the salmon on that river. While a huge amount of the electricity needed by Oregon and Washington comes from hydroelectric dams, these four dams produce just five percent of it. That five percent can be made up by using energy more wisely. It can also be made up by using other renewable energy sources. These options would create about 15,000 new jobs. New irrigation methods could keep the farmers in business.

So why not start saving the salmon by removing these Snake River dams? It would be good for the fish, good for people, and good for the economy. Plus, there's no good reason not to tear the dams down. So let's quit arguing about it. It's time to take action and save the salmon.

12. Summarize the arguments for removing the four Snake River dams.

___

___

___

___

___

___

___

13. The opening paragraphs of the article explain the history of the dams on the Columbia River system. Write a summary of this information.

A Penny's Worth

1 More pennies are produced and used than any other coin. Why? Do we really need pennies for anything? Don't you think it's time to get rid of them? Apparently a lot of people don't. Recent surveys show that about two-thirds of Americans want to keep the penny. There doesn't seem to be any good reason for their preference other than a longing to hold onto something familiar.

2 Why discontinue the penny? There are lots of reasons. To begin with, they're worth almost nothing. After all, what can you buy for a penny? Can you think of anything besides penny candy that can be bought for one cent?

3 Not only can you not buy anything with them, pennies really aren't worth much. Unlike some coins, pennies aren't made of a valuable metal. Before 1982, they were 95 percent copper and 5 percent zinc. Copper is slightly valuable, and at times in the 1970s people actually hoarded pennies. They hoped that the price of copper might go up so that all those useless pennies could be melted down and sold for

actual money. Then in 1982, the government changed the makeup of the penny. Now it's 97.6 percent zinc and 2.4 percent copper. That much zinc isn't worth a penny. So even the fleeting dream of a copper shortage no longer justifies the existence of pennies.

4 Today, pennies are just something to stick in your pocket and try to get rid of. And they're like rabbits: they just keep multiplying. Then what do you do with them? Even a whole handful of pennies isn't worth much.

5 Now think about all the useful places you *can't* use them at all. Vending machines and public transportation won't take them. And what if you accumulate a whole bunch of them—say, ten dollars worth? Most banks won't take them, unless you collect them into coin rolls first. You can't spend them in many stores. Cashiers aren't going to take the time to count 1,000 pennies. If they'll take them at all, they'll demand they be put in paper rolls first. That's a lot of trouble for $10.00, don't you think?

6 And both store owners and shoppers ought to hate pennies. It takes time to count out pennies when making a purchase and giving change. The National Association of Convenience Stores did a study. They estimated that it takes between two and two and one-half seconds to hunt through a handful of change and count out pennies every time someone makes a purchase. Maybe that doesn't sound like much, but consider all the purchases made every day. For example, by the time customers make one million purchases, those 2.5 seconds add up to more than 29 days. That's a lot of time spent counting out pennies! On a more personal level, imagine the time people would save standing in checkout lines if pennies were eliminated.

7 Of course, there's the flip side to the debate. If pennies were discontinued, what do you think stores would do with an item priced at $2.98? Do you think they'd round it down to $2.95 or up to $3.00? Some experts think the prices would go up, leading to higher prices across the board. They may be right, but so what? Even if every item you buy in a year goes up two cents, is that going to make a lot of difference to you? Try this experiment. For a week, don't give any pennies in change and collect all those you're given. At the end of the week, count up your pennies and multiply them by 52. That's about how much more you'd spend in a year if every item were rounded up to the nearest nickel. Now think about this: Is it worth that much to save you the trouble of dealing with all those pennies for a year? If you're like a lot of people, you'll think that rounding up is money well spent.

8 So the question is, why do we still have the penny? There seem to be few good reasons to continue minting them and passing them from one person to another. The U.S. military stopped using them at overseas military bases in the 1980s. Hardly anyone complained. So here's a suggestion. Let's eliminate them at home too. It'll be a simpler, happier world if we can do away with one of life's daily annoyances.

14. In paragraph three, the writer says that "pennies really aren't worth much." What three facts does the writer give to support this statement?

15. In paragraph six, the writer claims that both store owners and shoppers ought to hate pennies. Give two facts and two opinions to support this opinion.